THE TWO OCEANS

The Two Oceans: A Personal Account of Life, Finance and Business Philosophies

---

Martin Tiongson

First edition

Typeset in 11,5 / 15pt Adobe Caslon Pro

Book cover design, typesetting, and interior illustrations by Barış Şehri *please visit* sehribookdesign.com *for more*

Paperback ISBN: 979-8-9920136-2-7
Hardcover ISBN: 979-8-9920136-3-4
eBook ISBN: 979-8-9920136-4-1

To our support systems — those who are there for us during the times of storm or drought.

Who looks outside, dreams; who looks inside, awakes. – Carl Jung

Financial and Legal Disclaimer

The information contained in this book is for general information purposes only. Any reliance you place on such information is strictly at your own risk. It is not intended to constitute legal or personal investment advice; and does not take your individual circumstances and financial situation into account. I encourage you to conduct your own due diligence; and seek assistance or professional advice from a qualified licensed investment or tax advisor. I am an amateur retail investor.

My opinions, views, and commentaries provided here may include errors or inaccuracies. In no event will I be liable for any direct loss, any loss of profits, any loss of savings, any indirect loss, or consequential loss whatsoever arising out of, or in connection with, the information from this book.

Foreword

Have you ever wanted to find a book that walks through the kinds of life questions you've found yourself pondering? If you're curious about how successful everyday entrepreneurs do it—*The Millionaire Next Door*, so to speak—buckle up. The author isn't some flashy celebrity sharing their experience, but an everyday human, neighbor, and friend, who forged their own path and found success early on.

What Martin has done with this book is genuinely impactful — building a wealth of knowledge into a collection of stories that is nothing short of impressive. With this being his second book, it's easy to immerse yourself in his writing, which opens the curtain into both his business experience and his perspective on life — paired with his ongoing search for happiness and fulfillment, something we can all relate to.

Martin takes a wide-scope perspective, drawing from ideologies, theories, history, beliefs, and ethics — wrapping it all together in a journey of discovery and curiosity. He isn't teaching, he is sharing. He isn't preaching; he's thoughtfully putting on paper his wisdom and understanding of his experiences. His process. His successes. His failures. And ultimately, what has led him to where he is today.

Martin is a calm, kind, and humble soul who isn't trying to impress anyone. He is methodical, vulnerable, and generous in what he shares. He doesn't hold back, and he does so with intention.

After many years as an entrepreneur, he decided to write — and finished his first book within the year, publishing it in 2024.

I spent nine years writing my debut memoir. I share that only to say: when Martin puts his mind to something, he gives it his full attention. Whether it's a business deal, a book, or being present with family and friends. If you ever get the chance to meet him, you'll understand exactly what I mean.

In a world where everything is competing for our attention, Martin seems to move differently — pushing through the noise rather than getting caught in it. Take your time with this book. See where it takes you. See what it pulls out of you. We're all on our own journey of self-discovery, looking for that moment of clarity, that piece of insight that sticks.

Take a breath, find a quiet space, and settle in for a calm walk through Martin's peaceful Japanese garden of life lived and learned. Look for the takeaways — one at a time. Give it your full attention. I know that's still something I'm working on too.

I'm honored that Martin asked me to write this foreword. Thank you, Martin. God bless.

With Love, Alex L. Konicke
Amazon Bestselling Author
Evil Among Us: A True Story of Surviving Tragedy Through Murder, Fire and Forgiveness

Contents

Prologue

Uisce

("ish-kih")

Water, like time, gives as well as takes. It's reach, far and wide. It represents many things across different disciplines and fields of study.

In analytical psychology, water is a common but potent symbol. It mirrors emotions. Calm water symbolizes inner peace and tranquility. Turbulent water, emotional intensity and turmoil. Murky water, repression of distressing thoughts and impulses.

Bodies of water mirror life's journey. Seas and oceans suggest the collective unconscious. Lakes and ponds, the personal unconscious. Rivers represent flow and movement between stages. Waterfalls, a release or catharsis, while rain, a beginning or renewal.

In therapy, water represents submersion — down into the hidden, mysterious, and unfathomable depths of the psyche that lie beneath the surface of conscious awareness.

It is believed that to achieve psychological wholeness, one must *descend* into the water of forgotten memories, desires, and archetypes.

In spirituality, water is a sacred element, revered for its divine transformative nature. It acts as a conduit bridging the physical and spirit realms, considered integral in healing meditation and cleansing rituals across different cultures.

In mythology, water holds significance as a life-giving and purifying substance. *Uisce,* the Irish word for water, was derived from Celtic folklore. It even forms the root of "whiskey", through the phrase *uisce beatha*, meaning "water of life".

In history, *uisce* has been regarded as a medicinal cure for ailments such as colic and smallpox. It was also used as a general solvent, tonic, internal anesthetic, and an early form of antiseptic in medieval monasteries during the Early Middle Ages.

Beyond alcohol, *uisce* traditionally refers to Ireland's vital natural resource, where thousands of ancient wells are honored for their life-sustaining water.

—

Off in the distance, I saw two whales circle each other, perhaps each from one of the two oceans. They represented for me the inside and the outside, consciousness and the unconscious, push and pull, *yin* and *yang*, and temperance — which means balance.

Part 1

The Present

Chapter 1

Birdsong, Bramble, Time for Tea

Meditations in Impermanence

Song

A flurry of bright, cheerful yellow darted across the window as I watched inside the Windjammer. Goldfinch, perhaps a hundred of them, scattered like a handful of rice thrown in the air. Happily, lightly they soared and swooped, gathered and scattered, some zooming ahead, others trailing, from stoic tree branches to blades of grass dancing in the wind. They seemed weightless, like feathers unencumbered by the gravity of the world. One perched atop a swaying teasel, tentative and contemplative.

All kinds of birds made this place their home, if only for the spring: Canada geese, Cooper's hawks, turkey vultures, barred owls, American robins, chickadees, and Anna's hummingbirds coexisted in a constant flow of push and pull. The ecosystem also supported bright green tree frogs, black squirrels, short-tailed shrews, voles, coyotes, and deer.

The goldfinch chirped and called to one another mid-air. Their song harmonized into nature's symphony orchestra, rivaling even the London Philharmonic. Their music reminded me of an Alan Watts quote:

"When a bird sings, it doesn't sing for the advancement of music, but if somebody stops to listen and is delighted, that's fine."

British-American writer and self-professed "philosophical entertainer" Alan Watts posited that the purpose of one's actions does not necessarily have to be in pursuit of an external goal like career development, financial gain, competition, or prominence. The goal can simply be to express one's nature. What one does is done for one's own sake, without the need for a specific or productive outcome.

Watts suggested that an act's inherent value lies in the act itself, not in what it might achieve externally. The act itself is the purpose, while appreciation of it is secondary. A bird sings simply because it has a song to sing, not for some larger purpose. Watts applied this idea to his own life. He spoke in the same spirit that a bird sings — not to gain followers, but to share his point of view.

I approached writing in the same way; just like some people take up gardening, soap-making, woodworking, or birdwatching.

Spark

In the Audubon Society, a spark bird is a bird that ignites a person's lifelong interest and passion for birdwatching. The moment is often an early, memorable encounter with a species. This can be triggered by the bird's appearance, behavior, or a specific event.

My spark bird is the red-winged blackbird — a sleek bird with feathers of deepest black, set off by a bold patch of red on its wing and a striking sliver of yellow at the wingtip. I didn't know what it was when I first sighted it, but its striking appearance (and the painterly epaulettes on its shoulders) immediately piqued my interest.

My red-winged blackbird fussed on a cattail as I walked down the gravel river trail. Confident and gregarious, he proclaimed, "Here I am."

In the same way, everyone has a spark, whatever it may be — a hobby, a pastime, a skill, a sport, a style. Each of us is called to find the spark that will ignite our interest and passion.

Bramble

Fruit trees grew in Sandie's orchard year-round, while vegetables were imbedded in a grid of plant boxes. The shrubs and trees announced the seasons according to their rhythm, one after another, as their fruits ripened and announced the harvest: raspberries and salmonberries in June, currants and blackberries in June and July, plums and peaches in July and August, apples and pears in September and October, and grapes and walnuts in October.

The harvested fruit had endless applications: jam thickened from currants and blackberries, prunes dehydrated from plums, canned fruit preserved from peaches and pears, and wine pressed from apples and grapes.

I picked and gathered wild blackberries from the bramble that grew recklessly in the summer. The verdant hedges spread untamed and wild, like unwanted weeds. Vines scattered in every direction that called to them, their thorns sharp as razors, ready to pierce skin and draw blood. At the right time, the prickly shrub's fruit was sweet, succulent, and delicate. Its dark juices would stain my clothing and shoes, just like the blood from my fingertips when they carelessly kissed the blackberry thorn.

Under the heavy heat of the sunlit sky, I used hedge shears to prune the vines.

Prune

"The vine's strength is being wasted on good but not great branches. No great wine was ever made from an unpruned vine."

Here, American author Dr. Henry Cloud presents an allegory of the grapevine used in distilling wine. The pruning paradox presents a profound truth: Growth requires loss. The healthiest people and businesses routinely cut away good things to make way for great ones.

Cloud shares his own perspective on an approach to growth: not how to add more, but how to cut away what's holding us back. He reveals why success depends not on what we start, but what we're brave enough to end. According to Dr. Cloud, "Completing an ending well creates psychological closure that fuels new beginnings."

And thus, a paradoxical truth: "Winter isn't failure — it's nature's necessary ending." A person or business's next level of growth isn't blocked by what they lack. It's buried under what they won't let go of.

On one particularly cold night, a biting air descended on Sandie's farm. Wrapped in a light sweater the following morning, I found that the tomatoes had died in the early frost. The damaged vines needed to be pruned to encourage new, green, and healthy growth.

Tea

The conifers stayed evergreen while the maples, oaks, and hickories exploded in color. A windstorm visited under the blanket of night; an atmospheric river in the sky that was prelude to a crisp morning of bright leaves draping the ground in a patchwork quilt.

The chill in the air called for a cup of tea, and a time for stillness and presence. Jars of dried leaves and powders lined the last row in the Community Food Co-op: Dandelion root, milk thistle, and nettles for detoxing. Lemon, ginger, and turmeric as anti-inflammatories and antioxidants. Chamomile, lavender, and peppermint for relaxation and sleep. A Japanese proverb chimed like a bell:

"Ichigo-Ichie."

The tea ceremony has long been a time-honored institution in Japan, rooted in the principles of Zen Buddhism and founded on the reverence for the beauty of everyday life. The custom is traditionally observed to welcome guests with great care.

Sen no Rikyu, a sixteenth century tea master, developed the art of the tea ceremony, codifying it into a style known as *wabi-cha* (emphasizing simplicity, quietude, and the absence of ornament), and elevated it into an art that encompassed rules of procedure, utensils, teahouse architecture, and tea-garden landscaping.

The Zen Buddhist principle known as *ichigo-ichie* translates to "one time, one meeting." It is a fundamental concept, teaching that every encounter, such as a tea ceremony, is a unique event that will never happen again in the exact same way. It encourages treasuring each moment and treating each human interaction as precious and irreplaceable. Because of their ephemeral and sacred nature, we should value all human connections and engage in them with sincerity and our full attention.

"When tea master Sen no Rikyu served tea to his guests, he moved with remarkable deliberation to honor the fact that the meeting could never be repeated or replicated. It was a once-in-a-lifetime experience."

Thus, when I have a cup of tea, I try to be mindful of being still and present in the moment. It is a moment in time that can't and never will be captured again.

I have gained appreciation for the simple act of preparing, steeping, and drinking tea in this way, whether at home or at a restaurant. Nothing means anything until we give meaning to it. And so, the meaning of life can be found in every small, quiet moment. Life is mundane, ordinary, and insignificant. But because the present will never happen again, it is temporal, fleeting, and precious.

Zen

Life is impermanent. Everything is transient. If you are interacting with someone and you are annoyed or in a bad mood, feel like judging them, or don't feel like listening to them, remember *ichigo-ichie*. They are giving you their most precious possession: their time, right now. By being present and listening, you can have a meaningful conversation and bring joy to you both. (I can bravely admit that I need to work on this myself.)

Zen principles teach mindfulness and presence, simplicity and detachment: Mindfulness and presence in daily activities — viewing them as opportunities for practice and awakening; and simplicity and detachment from material possessions and worldly desires — promoting a focus on inner experience.

Zen teaches "Four Noble Truths": (1) Human life entails a lot of suffering. (2) The cause of suffering is desire (attachment, craving, greed, the pain of an unlived life). (3) It is possible to end suffering. (4) The path to end suffering is to follow the Middle Way (not to live a life of excessive indulgence and luxury, or a life of excessive fasting and hardship).

A teacher once told me that they had good news and bad news: Everything is temporary and nothing lasts forever. Thus, if you *are* happy now, that feeling will end at some point. And in the same way, if you are *not* happy now, that feeling will also end at some point.

I put on my hat and coat, stepped outside the door, and took to the gently winding road. A gust of wind lifted errant leaves and spun them around in the air. I paused for a moment and mused: The maples, oaks, and hickories will reunite with the conifers in the green of spring.

A spark ignites.

Chapter 2

A Cat Named Thor

The Reciprocity of Kindness with Empathy

The Foster Cat

The Human drove to the cat center to pick up Thor, a tabby cat of around ten years old. The door swung open as the Human entered its premises. On the floor lay a small, old, inconsequential-looking carrier. But inside it was a cat. Ellie, a British woman who volunteered at the cat center, informed the Human that they had gotten Thor from an animal shelter. The elderly cat had been there for a long time but was not adopted. If the cat center had not taken him, he might have been euthanized. She thanked the Human for taking care of the cat and giving him a safe place to stay until they could find a good owner for him.

The Human picked up the forest-green carrier by its handle and carried it to his car. On the way home, he noticed that Thor was quiet as a mouse, which was curious. All the other cats the Human had fostered before had meowed loudly throughout the drive, voicing their displeasure at traveling with a stranger to an unfamiliar place.

The Human had always tried to reassure them, doing his best to make the drive as smooth and comfortable as possible.

The First Week

Arriving home, the Human set down the carrier on the floor and opened its stainless-steel gate. Thor did not move. He just stayed inside, peering out with his big round eyes. He was lying on a terry cloth towel, his only material possession and source of comfort in the world. This was the first time the Human got a good look at the cat. He was gray with black tiger stripes and clean white mittens. A smudge of white on his nose looked like the stroke of a brush, as if he were an artist who accidentally got wet paint on his face.

The Human went into a different room so Thor could exit his little hutch on his own terms. After a couple of hours, the Human found that the tabby cat had not budged an inch. He wondered, *who named you Thor? You are very timid and not Thor-like at all.*

Zip ties secured the top half of the carrier to the bottom, so the Human gently tipped the old carrier onto its side to coax out the small tabby. Thor slinked out of the container like molasses and in short order proceeded to take sanctuary under a nearby couch. *He will come out of hiding when he feels it is safe,* thought the Human. So, he left a food dish, a water bowl, and a litter box next to the couch.

The night came and went. After fourteen hours, Thor was still under the couch. He didn't come out for anything — not even to eat, drink or use the litter box. Cats are known to take the path of least resistance. So, the Human decided it was time to intervene. He moved the couch and picked up the soft little animal nestled against the wall. For some reason, Thor did not try to run away. He uttered soft little meows but thankfully decided not to resort to violence.

Thor and the Human sat together enclosed in the small bathroom. It turned out that the cat just needed positive reinforcement. After an hour of the Human reassuring him, Thor decided to take some nourishment in the form of wet food and relieve himself in the litter box. After that, the Human let Thor out of the bathroom.

The Human's home was a small, quiet place, ideal for a cat. Thor was free to roam as he pleased. Now that he felt safe, the little gray tabby was no longer afraid to serenade during the midnight hours. He seemed to be searching for something or someone.

The Second Week

As it turned out, Thor was a healthy eater who was thankfully not picky about his food. His regular meals consisted of wet food in yellow pouches. His favorites were salmon and tuna, but he also indulged in other varieties. He liked chicken pâté on occasion, but not all the time.

He ate around nine ounces per day, consisting of six meals of 1.5 ounces (equivalent to three 3-ounce pouches). The Human gave him small portions so his wet food would remain fresh. Thor's favorite treats were freeze-dried chicken and lickable tubes. He also had a penchant for human food like shredded chicken and pieces of ham. He would inspect what the Human was eating and demand a taste.

He had access to dry food all the time, but Thor would only eat that if he got hungry. This was perfect because his primary source of nutrition had to be healthy wet food. He also had bowls of clean water available to him around the clock, scattered about like miniature ponds. The water was replaced once a day. He lapped at it occasionally, mostly when it was hot or if the Human was away.

Thankfully, Thor was easy, unlike Buzz. Buzz was a female tabby who had been put on a strict diet by the cat center. But she simply decided not to indulge any of their foolish shenanigans. They tried feeding her beef, chicken, duck, lamb, mackerel, salmon, shrimp, tuna, deer, mouse, rabbit, venison, and beaver. They tried different forms like chunks, morsels, shreds, pâté, and gravy. However, she would only eat Temptations, which was the equivalent of junk food for cats, and nothing else. Buzz did not cover her litter, as if to say, *not my problem.* And the sociopathic feline had the audacity to sharpen her murder weapons without breaking eye contact.

In contrast, Thor appreciated his tidy surroundings. He covered his litter and always called the Human to come clean it right away. He also had a funny habit of digging at the floor after eating. It was his way of saying: *I'm done now. Take this away so as not to attract any predators.*

The Following Weeks

Familiarity grows over time. Like Zen masters, cats also thrive on the three Rs: routine, ritual, and rhythm. Thor had a friendly personality and calm disposition when he felt safe. He liked belly rubs and chin scratches. He preferred being close to humans and tolerated being picked up and carried. But he would still occasionally get scared by noises and strangers.

Thor's playful side soon started to emerge. He was fond of catnip kickers, lasers, wands, and horizontal scratching boxes. One of his favorite playthings was an electronic motion toy with a concealed rotating wand. Thor's playfulness was of a polite sort, unlike Luna, a mischievous tuxedo cat who liked to knock things off shelves and tables (and had to be given an appetite stimulant by syringe). With her antics, Luna was a comforting remedy for the lonely and emotionally adrift. Her Human became accustomed to her constant presence. She was there every time a cupboard was opened, every time a room was entered, every time a car pulled into the driveway.

Though he still exhibited a youthful exuberance, Thor's age was apparent in the finer details. He didn't jump onto high surfaces or scratch vertical posts. He favored his one side due to arthritis, and one leg had been shaved for an IV, the Human assumed. Most of the time, Thor preferred to be on the ground, but he could jump on the bed, couch, low tables, or windowsills with some effort.

He was not an aggressive or destructive cat at all. He didn't scratch furniture or destroy indoor plants. And with time, Thor's confidence grew. He began to enjoy spending afternoons on the patio, lazing about, or sitting on the windowsill to watch birds and squirrels.

Still, he was the opposite of Blaine, another tabby who belonged to the Human's neighbor. Blaine was a very confident and intelligent cat. He was owned by an older gentleman, and Blaine would sometimes get locked out of his house. However, he always knew where it was. When the Human became his friend, Blaine would guide and nudge him to push his front door open so he could get back inside around dusk when it was time to go home. He would sometimes hop on the fence and sit there, or he would stand outside the Human's bedroom window. He would tap on the glass, knowing that he might get a treat. Sometimes, the Human would come home and see Blaine's bell-shaped silhouette in the dark, where he sat patiently in the street. He would think to himself, *Blaine, did you get yourself locked out again?*

The Night Hours

Like most cats, Thor was nocturnal. He was like Kiwi, a sleek black cat who kept to an organized routine and a strict regimen.

Every afternoon, Kiwi napped on top of a pile of freshly laundered clothes in a hamper in the closet in the guest bedroom. And at night, he curled up beside his Human on a warm, safe bed. With his peaceful rhythm, Kiwi offered quiet, unhurried companionship. And a safe for life's secrets.

Thor adjusted to his new environment surprisingly fast. His favorite spot was a warm, fluffy cat bed under the Human's bed. The Human could reach out to Thor while he was hiding there without getting scratched or swiped at. If called, Thor would come out of his secret spot with an expression on his face that said, *Is it time for dinner yet?*

One night, the Human had a horrible nightmare. It seemed to go on without end. As he sank deeper into the pit of the nightmare, he started to hear soft little meows. When he came to, he found Thor sitting beside him in the dark. It was as if the small cat had heard the commotion and proceeded to coax the Human from his terrors.

Attunement is being aware of, responsive to, and in harmony with another. Thor, an observant cat, acted as a calming anchor. It turned out that the Human needed positive reinforcement as well, and he felt safe with Thor in his environment.

The human nervous system is wired for predictability and subtlety. In their still moments of shared silence, Thor proffered presence without pressure, comfort without judgment, and connection that didn't demand constant output.

The Adoption

Several months later, the Human received the inevitable call from the cat center. Thor had waited a very long time, going back to his time at the animal shelter and even before that. But it was time to bring him in. Thor had finally been adopted.

The Human found it difficult to say goodbye to the cat. How could he communicate that this would be the last time they would see each other? How could he articulate that Thor was a good cat and not to be afraid? He was going to his forever home, where he would spend the rest of his days. All the Human could do was think reassuring thoughts and blink slowly. This sad moment was temporary, ephemeral. Everything would be well soon.

The Human gently ushered the gray tabby into the small carrier. Thor went inside his former home silently and without any complications. The Human wished he could pack everything for Thor, but he understood that the cat would eventually have his own things when he finally got to go home.

With a big sigh, the Human picked up the carrier once more and placed it on the passenger seat. As he was driving, something unexpected happened. To his surprise, Thor kept meowing loudly and repeatedly the whole drive to the cat center. His vocalizations were like tiny strikes of thunder. Thor lived up to his namesake in that moment.

It appeared that over the last few months, he had regained his will and energy to express himself, even his dissatisfaction. This was in sharp contrast to his behavior during the drive from the cat center, when he had no fight left in him and had seemingly given up on life. The cat center didn't know Thor's history, but the Human surmised that the gray tabby had seen his fair share of trials and tribulations.

Goodbye Before Hello

There was no available parking near the cat center, so the Human had to park several blocks away and carry the cat carrier all the way there. He didn't know if it was because of the distance, or if Thor had gained some weight, but the carrier seemed much heavier than before. A big mess of road construction was happening outside on the street, where a worker was jackhammering away. As he passed him, the Human mentally apologized to the cat for the loud, scary noises in this unfamiliar place.

The Human and Thor entered the cat center, and Ellie was there to greet them. She opened the carrier as they talked. Thor slipped out as inconspicuously as he could and crawled into a small enclosure to hide away. All around them were cats of different ages, breeds, colors, and temperaments: Loudmouth, Clover, Oregano, Tabby, and Callie. The cats didn't ask humans to perform or test their loyalty, and they didn't confuse intensity with intimacy. They simply settled into a space to coexist with them, which was more than enough.

Meanwhile, a large flock of pigeons congregated outside the two window walls like a council of tricksters, there to taunt the adoptable and resident cats, who could only plot their demise from the other side.

The Human wrote a letter that outlined his foster notes and experiences with Thor in the brief time they shared together — including his likes, dislikes, habits, and peculiarities. He handed Ellie the letter to give to the gray tabby's new owner. As he drove back, he imagined Thor's future life to be happy and safe, filled with the love and kindness he deserved, in a home with a warm, fluffy bed, a patio, and a windowsill for watching squirrels and birds.

That is the miracle of cats. They live not in past memory but in the present moment: *I am cat. I am hungry; therefore, I will eat. I am sleepy; therefore, I will nap. I feel safe sharing this space with this other being. This place is my territory; therefore, I will patrol it. This spot is comfortable; therefore, this is where I shall be.*

Be Like a Cat

When a cat falls out of a tree, it lets go of itself. The cat becomes completely relaxed, and lands lightly on the ground. But if a cat were about to fall out of a tree and suddenly makes up its mind that it didn't want to fall, it would become tense and rigid. And would be just a bag of bones upon landing.
In the same way, it is the philosophy of the Tao that we are falling off a tree, at every moment of our lives. As a matter of fact, the moment we were born, we were kicked off a precipice and we are falling. And there is nothing that can stop it.
So instead of living in a state of chronic tension and clinging to all sorts of things that are falling with us because the whole world is impermanent, be like a cat.
– Alan Watts, *What Is Tao?*

Philosofur, the cat.

Chapter 3

A Trainwreck of a Trip

A Practice of Control

The Surprise Passengers

I was waiting for my flight at the airport when I felt a gentle tap on my shoulder. It was the kids of a couple of new acquaintances of mine. The two young adults, bags in tow, had a spark of recognition in their eyes and greeted me with friendly smiles. "Yes, it is me," I said. They had missed their flight to Miami, and had been bumped to mine, which was later in the day. It was one of the strangest and most random coincidences in my life. This was to be the first real vacation I took after I left my job of almost ten years. And this was their first ever trip to Florida. What were the chances that I would be going to the same place at the same time as some people I just met? It had to be kismet.

As we boarded the plane, we found that we were all even seated in the same row. Because they missed their original flight, their transportation arrangements in Miami had also changed. They would have been picked up at the airport. Instead, their car would wait at their Airbnb. Because of this, they needed a way to get from the airport to the Airbnb. They asked if I could drive them there. I thought it wouldn't be a big deal. I also felt obligated to do it because they were a couple of kids, and I wanted to make sure they were okay. Still, I really needed to wind down, decompress, and get away — the goal of this vacation.

After landing, we briskly walked to the rental car center, and I checked in at the counter. I was instructed to head to the garage, where the parking attendant handed me a key to one of the vehicles. Our brief interaction entailed nothing out of the ordinary: just standard pleasantries.

The I-95 in South Florida is already horrible at any given time of day, but it happened to be rush hour as well. The traffic congestion was insane. Bumper-to-bumper on the freeway, the cars were completely stationary most of the time. And if they moved, it was at a glacial pace. Surprisingly, there were no road accidents. This was just standard fare for a weekday in metro South Florida. Floridian drivers had a reputation. They had two modes: fast and reckless, or excruciatingly slow. I was deliberately more cautious and defensive while driving, so I wouldn't get in an accident. It took four hours to drive to the kids' place and back to my hotel, on top of the six-hour flight.

The Forgotten Luggage

I had not lived in Miami for thirteen years. It was drastically different from how I remembered it in 2012. It was completely unrecognizable to me. It felt like I had traveled to someplace I had never been before. I remembered once watching the story of a homeowner who refused to sell their property because they didn't want to part with their cherished family home. And so, a mixed-use development was built around it. The little house got boxed in by the new skyscrapers and the tall shadows they cast. Somehow, this was what it felt like.

The next day, I awoke to a flurry of messages and missed calls. One of the kids had left their bag in my rental car. They asked if I could deliver it to them. I responded that they could drive to where I was staying. Even though I didn't drive to them, I had to postpone my own plans and work around their schedule. We arranged a time to meet, and I waited for them so I could return their missing luggage. Sorting out this small dilemma took up most of my day.

With the incident out of the way, I made plans to meet my friend and former mentor, Andy, and his wife, Susie, at their home. Andy had paved the way for me to get my first internship, which led to me opening my first brokerage account (which I am very thankful for today). It would be a good opportunity to reconnect after a long time. It had been more than ten years since we last saw each other.

The Stalled Rental Car

I left the hotel at around 11 a.m. I was on the way to Andy and Susie's house when I noticed that the fuel gauge was low. I was surprised at how quickly the fuel was depleting; *it couldn't have been a very fuel-efficient car*. I stopped at a gas station and got out of the car to refill the tank. I searched for the fuel cap and saw that there was none. It was only then that I realized I was driving an electric car (and not even a hybrid).

I was caught by surprise. I had never driven an electric car before, so I had no clue that I was driving one. What I had thought was the fuel gauge was in fact the state of charge (SOC) gauge. The attendant at the rental car center had not said anything to me when he handed me the key to the vehicle.

I asked at the gas station and the auto shop next door if there were any Hyundai charging stations nearby. I searched for one on my phone as well. There was none. On top of that, traffic was horrible as usual. The auto shop could not help me either. The car would run empty and stall before I could reach a charging station, if there were any.

Meanwhile, I still had a lunch meeting to go to. I sent Andy several updates with my apologies. I thought I could still make it, that I would just be running late, but I never got there. I realized later that they had prepared a meal for me, which is something I still feel guilty about.

The Gas Station

It was a hot, sweltering Florida day. With the car parked at the gas station, I called the rental car company, and they confirmed that there were no charging stations in my area. The person on the line apologized and agreed that I should have been told from the beginning that I was being handed an electric vehicle — as was their official company policy.

We formed a plan to have the car towed: The tow truck would drive me and the car to Miami Airport. The car would be dropped off there, and I would simply walk to the rental car center to get a replacement. I agreed to this course of action, which seemed reasonable and efficient.

They told me they could call a tow truck for me, but that I would have to pay out of pocket for it (even though the fault was theirs). This was because the tow truck company was a different entity from the rental car company. I could pay for the tow truck upfront, then submit a complaint to the rental company and request a reimbursement for the charges later. I relented because I was tired and hungry.

I wanted to reach a resolution on this trainwreck of a trip as soon as possible.

I was sure to tell the support agent that I wanted a gas-powered vehicle instead of an electric vehicle this time. It was impossible to drive an EV without it dying because of the traffic congestion and lack of Hyundai charging stations in the city. The agent agreed.

The Tow Truck

There was nothing to do but wait. I sat on the curb outside the gas station convenience store. I didn't want to stray too far, so I could flag down the tow truck when it arrived.

I received a few calls from the driver. He informed me that he would be towing the car to an address given to him by the rental company — which was *not* at the airport. He said that I didn't need to wait for him and to just leave the key inside the unlocked car (I was wary of this plan), and that I would need to find my own way to the rental car center at Miami Airport. I chalked it up to miscommunication, or maybe it was a language barrier issue. The conversations I had with him were not clear to me. The person I had talked to at the rental company had clearly told me that the car lot was next to the rental car center, at Miami Airport. I called the rental company again to verify. This time I spoke to a different agent, but I was told the same thing. I called the tow truck driver back, and he insisted that they had given him a different address. I asked if I could still ride with him to the car lot. He said that was fine. I figured that I would just let everything play out. The worst had to be over, surely things couldn't get any worse.

After more than two hours of waiting, the tow truck finally arrived. I was feverish and sweaty from being out in the sun. The tow truck driver repeated that he would be going to a car lot that was *not* at the airport. However, the rental company had confirmed multiple times that the car lot and the airport rental car center were in the same location.

I hopped in the tow truck. Unsurprisingly, traffic was once again horrendous. It took about an hour to reach our destination. At this point, it was almost 5 p.m. As we got closer, it dawned on me that the tow truck driver had been right all along. The address that the car rental company had given him was an impound lot. I didn't know where it was relative to the airport, but I could tell that it was nowhere near it.

The Impound Lot

The car was impounded at the lot. I asked the driver if he could drive me to the airport. He answered with a resounding no and went on his way. I sat down on the curb. Garage cats were sauntering all around, but they were skittish with strangers. Once again, I called the car rental company. My phone's battery was now running low. They confirmed what I already knew: The car lot was not at the airport, and there were no rental car centers nearby.

The support agent said they could assist me by calling an Uber to take me to the airport. I did not have the ridesharing app on my phone. I told them that they needed to pay for the Uber after their abundance of mistakes and undelivered promises. They relented and escalated the matter to their supervisor, who begrudgingly approved my request. The Uber arrived shortly after and drove me to the address provided by the car rental company.

Miami Airport

The Uber dropped me off at what appeared to be a train terminal. *(Oh no, not again.)* I asked a nearby security officer for directions. I found that I was indeed at the airport, but the car rental center was still a good distance away. I obtained directions and proceeded to walk there.

There were three employees at the car rental center. All of them seemed over it before I even approached them. I knew I had to tread lightly. There was one customer ahead of me. When my turn came, I slowly explained my situation and what I needed from them. I tried to be as concise as I could. Though their demeanor was not the most cordial, they were at least knowledgeable. They understood what I was trying to accomplish. They checked the computer to see if there were any available cars (since I did not have a reservation). That was when the senior employee among them hit me with a gut punch — they only had electric vehicles available. *(You have got to be kidding me.)* Like a mage sending a knight on a quest, she offered a possible solution. I could take one of the available electric cars and drive it to Fort Lauderdale Airport. There, I could possibly replace it with a gas-powered car.

I asked if there was a way for them to confirm that they had a gas-powered vehicle available at Fort Lauderdale. I would hate to drive all the way there and come back with nothing. She said no, their system only lets them see their location's inventory. The corporate office would not know if I called them either. Only the specific location could see their inventory. I figured I would take my chances. *The tenth circle of hell is this trip to Florida*, I grumbled to myself.

I confess that I was just sick of electric cars at this point. Based on this experience, I felt that an electric car only makes sense if you use it for work, have a regular routine, and have a charging station nearby. It's a different story when you are traveling and you are not familiar with the rental vehicle, the lay of the land, the traffic conditions, and the locations of charging stations. It can end up being very stressful for an unsavvy traveler such as myself. It didn't help that the phone I had at the time was also an obsolete, laggy model.

Fort Lauderdale Airport

It took another couple of hours to reach Fort Lauderdale Airport. After such a long, grueling day where nothing went right and I endured one ordeal after another, I finally received some good news: a gas-powered vehicle was available. I traded in the electric car and drove back to my hotel. By then, it was close to 10 p.m. I accomplished nothing for the day.

I rescheduled my lunch with Andy and Susie for the following day. They both graciously accepted my apology. I left early so I would not be late. I arrived in the area a few hours early, so I took the time to explore, get reacquainted with my old neighborhood, and enjoy the sunny weather. I even bought a book from the same Barnes & Noble I used to frequent. It was still there after all that time.

After this ordeal, I gave my body permission to give in to the resulting fatigue and exhaustion. I felt unwell for the remainder of the trip. My finger also got swollen, possibly due to an infection. Interestingly, that happened to me twice, and both times were in Florida. At least the swelling went away on its own this time. And I didn't have to see a hand doctor like the time before.

Stoicism

I look back on this series of unfortunate events as a test in stoicism, a Hellenistic philosophy dating back to ancient Greece and Rome.

Stoicism focuses on developing inner resilience and self-control. Things that are external are outside of my control — the acquaintances' kids, the rental car attendant, the traffic, the heat, the support agent, the tow truck driver, the inventory of gas-powered vehicles. What I can control are my own thoughts, feelings, decisions, and responses to outside stimuli.

Human society is an interwoven system of complicated roles and relationships, common interests and beliefs. This means that most things are outside of your control. You can only navigate its unending complexities to the best of your ability.

There are times in life when misfortune begets more misfortune. But each obstacle you overcome, each challenge you confront leads to eventual resolution, even if you don't know it at the time. All you can do is take things in your stride and keep on pushing.

Sonder is every window, each with a person inside writing their own story.

Chapter 4

Zorro at the Balboa

A Place for Virtues

One brisk Monday night, I had nothing better to do, so I decided to see what was playing at the Balboa Theatre — a historic landmark and community performing arts gem in the region. It was designed by architect William Wheeler and first opened as a vaudeville and cinema theatre in March 1924. In 1996, it was listed on the National Register of Historic Places, and in 2008, it was refurbished with a tiled dome and Baroque fretwork before reopening as a performing arts venue.

The Balboa Theatre featured a variety of shows, plays, and performances, from live music by a David Bowie tribute band one day, to a showing of *The Big Lebowski* with a panel discussion with Jeff Bridges the next.

On this night, it was a screening of the 1920 silent movie *The Mark of Zorro* starring the indomitable Douglas Fairbanks. The black-and-white film was going to be accompanied by a live organ played by Ken Double. The theatre was only a short walk from the apartment I was staying in, and since it was a weeknight, the walk was easy, with only a sprinkling of people downtown. I reached my destination and bought my ticket from the languid booking clerk who idly sat inside the ticket booth. I made my way past the security checkpoint to my seat in the storied auditorium. The theatergoers looked sharp, dressed to the nines for a night at the theatre, like back in the day. Some of the patrons were even on theme, decked out in their Roaring Twenties best, wearing tuxedos and sparkling, beaded gowns.

As the silent movie started, I was once again reminded of the impermanence and temporary nature of things. Everything can and will change. *The Mark of Zorro* was filmed over a hundred years ago. All the players were long gone. All that remained was what was preserved on the cellulose. In a sense, the movie was a hundred-minute excursion to a bygone era.

It invoked in me an eerie feeling of familiarity, as I confronted this unreachable distance to the past that I couldn't hold on to or reach ever again. All that remained were the memories and reminders, the mementos and souvenirs that I could only watch as a bystander. Does anything else remain?

The Four Stoic Virtues

Summum bonum was an expression used by Cicero, Rome's greatest orator. In Latin, it means "the highest good." What is the highest good? What is it that we are supposed to be aiming for in this life? *What remains?* To the stoics, the answer was virtue. They said that everything we face in life, even bad, painful, or scary situations, is an opportunity to respond with virtue. They believed if we act virtuously, everything good would follow: happiness, honor, love, reputation, success, meaning. "The man who has virtue is in need of nothing whatever for the purpose of living well." A virtuous person needs nothing else for fulfillment. (The Daily Stoic)

Wisdom, justice, courage, and temperance are the four stoic virtues. Central to stoic philosophy, they serve as a guide for living a meaningful, ethical, and resilient life.

Wisdom

The prudence to understand the world logically and without prejudice.

The theater's pipe organ was large and imposing, taking a big space in the orchestra pit. It was painted in glorious gold and candy-apple red. The organist matched the showmanship of his towering instrument by wearing a glittering suit and sequined shoes to match. He looked larger than life, even several feet away from where I sat.

Ken Double played with great precision and synchronicity with the images on the silver screen. His music perfectly matched and elevated every scene that unfolded, accentuating every emotion the actors conveyed and punctuating every mood the story evoked.

He only had three sheets of paper in front of him for the whole hundred-minute film, which contained just eleven themes. Mr. Double accompanied the scenes by building upon, mixing, taking apart, and improvising on those eleven themes for the whole duration of the movie.

It was an impressive and awe-inspiring example of what a person can achieve when they dedicate their life to honing their craft and controlling the things that they can, such as their own skills, talents, and abilities. Wisdom is knowing, learning, and having the experiences required to navigate the world.

Justice

The fairness to treat others according to the Golden Rule, that which involves social equality and what is right for the community.

The movie's central themes dealt with oppression and justice: the idealistic and unkillable hope that a hero would rise to serve justice to the people in power who take advantage of the disadvantaged, and to champion the oppressed. Justice means defending what's right, even at great personal risk. It is a virtue that resonates through time, still holding its place and purpose in the various decades and incarnations of society since.

As a film, *The Mark of Zorro* has stood the test of time even after more than a century. I marveled at the actors' athleticism and comedic timing. I laughed at the charming humor of the last scene. The audience audibly reacted to the chase and fight scenes that were carefully choreographed like a highly technical dance. The intertitles struck a chord with everyone present: "Justice for all! Punishment for the oppressors of the helpless, from the governor down."

"No force that tyranny could bring would dare oppose us, once united. Our country's out of joint. It is for us *caballeros*, and us alone, to set it right!" The audience erupted in rapture cheering at the long-awaited catharsis. It felt like receiving a message in a bottle hurled across time that has finally washed ashore one hundred years later. It was as if it came from someplace far away, from someone who lived similar experiences and shared our ideals, hopes, and dreams.

Courage

The fortitude to face challenges and persevere, particularly in the face of fear.

"The heaven-kissed hills of your native California swarm with the sentinels of oppression! Are your pulses dead? Thank God, mine is not. And I pledge you; my blood's as noble as the best!"

Zorro's tale is deeply ingrained in California. The very fabric of California is woven through the legend of Zorro, including its Spanish Colonial history, colliding cultures, and fervent dreams. But its tapestry has extended beyond state lines through the generations of weavers that followed — formidable creators, authors, and playwrights who have been inspired to write stories that they have made their own. I felt motivated even as I circulated the balcony lounge during the intermission.

The Mark of Zorro is considered the grandfather of the superhero genre. One can clearly see the direct influence it has had on archetypes, characters, conflicts, and plot structures created since, such as *Batman*. After the tragic murder of his parents, Bruce Wayne made it his brave mission to rid his beloved City of Gotham of the scourge of crime and the blight of corruption. Courage means overcoming our own fears and going on our own hero's journey; to change the things we can control and influence.

Temperance

The self-discipline to restrain from excess and find moderation between extremes.

Douglas Fairbanks, known as "The King of Hollywood", made his mark on history primarily through his pioneering work as a founding member of United Artists and the Academy of Motion Picture Arts and Sciences. He helped create a new model for filmmaking and establish standards for a whole genre of films. He achieved these notable accomplishments through temperance: doing the right thing in the right amount in the right way. Temperance implies balance, which is a virtue worth continuously striving for.

In 1919, Fairbanks co-founded United Artists with Charlie Chaplin, Mary Pickford, and D.W. Griffith, creating a distribution company for their independently produced films. This move was revolutionary, as it gave artists greater creative control and ownership over their work, shifting power away from the major studios.

In 1927, he became a founding member of the Academy of Motion Picture Arts and Sciences. He even hosted the first Academy Awards ceremony in 1929, helping to shape the industry's prestigious awards tradition.

Fairbanks also pioneered film education by collaborating on the establishment of the first university bachelor's degree program in cinema, which was created at the University of Southern California. He employed temperance, in the right place at the right time.

In addition to starring in *The Mark of Zorro*, he played the title characters in *Robin Hood* (1922), *The Thief of Baghdad* (1924), *The Black Pirate* (1926), and *The Iron Mask* (1929).

In Sum

Mr. Double held a short talk after the movie to discuss his process. There was a hush in the auditorium as he spoke. I listened intently. It was one of those nights that stick out in my memory. I walked back home under the warm colored lights of the cool California night. I glanced at the open windows of apartment buildings on both sides of the street. Inside, people were illuminated by the glow of their TV screens, each living out their own stories.

I have moved out of that apartment and that city since. I'm uncertain that I will ever get to relive those same experiences — walking on the waterfront, watching a Padres game at Petco Park, seeing a show at the Civic Theater, going to the Gaslamp Quarter with its speakeasies and collection of comedy and jazz clubs, eating the best pizza in Little Italy. Everything is good while it lasts.

Time has value, so it's important to use it wisely. We are urged to make the most of the present moment. It can be easy to get caught up in planning for the future or dwelling on the past. But fleeting moments become cherished memories. By focusing on the present and accepting things as they are, we can find more peace and contentment in life.

Like time, many things in life are beyond our control. Stoicism encourages us to focus our efforts on cultivating inner virtues and improving our selves, which is within our power, rather than striving to change our external circumstances.

Our virtues linger. They echo through time even after we are long gone.

"All the world's a stage,
And all the men and women merely players.
They have their exits and their entrances,
And one man in his time plays many parts,
His acts being seven ages."
– William Shakespeare, As You Like It, Act II, Scene VII

Chapter 5

Whales Outside Our Windows

A Perspective on Plato's View

La Paz

I parked my car at CBX, crossed the border to Tijuana, and flew from there to Baja California Sur. My first trip to Mexico was for a whale-watching expedition organized by Jeffrey Lehmann, host and producer of the PBS travel series, *Weekend Explorer*. My destination was La Paz, a shimmering coastal city that gave me a renewed sense of hope. It is a place of peace, true to its name.

Stepping onto the Malecón, I reveled in the sights and sounds of La Paz's waterfront boardwalk. The capital has a rich history, told through the statues and landmarks on the promenade. A restaurant nearby had a pulley system to transport pizza and drinks across from another building that housed its kitchen. And impressively, not a slice or drop was spilled.

There on the rooftop, I witnessed the most thought-provoking sunset. The sky moved from the friendly greeting of yellow, to the bright gaze of orange, to the violent intensity of red, to the tender caress of pink, to the melancholy embrace of purple, and finally, to the sobering farewell of midnight blue. The color composition on the horizon changed every minute. In that moment, I pondered how our emotions and lives can suddenly shift, even in a short timespan like a parting sunset.

I sipped an espresso martini at the Azotea atop the República Pagana — an establishment so renowned that it needed no signage. It just *was*.

La Ventana

The next day, I took a shuttle at dawn to La Ventana, which translates to "The Window". It is a fitting description of the picturesque fishing village. While sailing on a pontoon, I spotted coastal wildlife — humpback whales, sea lions, and mountain goats that stood tall on the crags on the coast. Mobula rays propelled themselves over the water, flapping their fins like wings. They eagerly sought to touch the sky and catch the clouds, even for a moment. They knew a whole world existed beyond their own horizon.

No words could do justice to the majesty of our planet. I felt fortunate to bear witness to these brief, gone-in-a-blink moments. The water gently lapped and cascaded. The sea was an ever-moving and forever-changing portrait, proof of the relentless march of time.

Pods of whales surfaced and descended. I saw them simply living in the present, in this strait, unconcerned about the future or the past. They swam through their own world of deep sea and sky, unfettered and free. Sea lions floated in the water, their fins clasped together in gentle sleep and group meditation. Others basked on the rocks in the glow of the midday sun, eyes closed and hearts open.

The wind visited La Ventana in the afternoons, and windsurfers were out in full force that day. They flocked to the beach, eager to meet the wind. A rainbow of kites dotted the cotton sky. From afar, they simply appeared to be caught in a gentle breeze. But up close, the gales were strong and thunderous, powerful enough to lift windsurfers and their boards several feet into the air.

It was a peaceful day both externally and internally in my mind. It made me wonder if the people I saw in the distance were happy, or if they were there to escape the gale-force winds of their own inner worlds.

The Sonoran Desert

The following day, I traversed the vast expanse of the Sonoran Desert. It stretched as far as the eye could see. Cacti stood motionless under the desert sun, moon, and stars, unmoved by time. I spotted a caracara perched on a mighty cactus. The bird of prey's neon-orange beak contrasted with the backdrop of olive-green desert flora. It lived in its own world of terracotta plains and azure skies. I imagined myself flying like one of them, with the world below nothing but a tiny speck. I could picture it clearly, its days spent gliding and casting a dark shadow over the desert sands.

The terrain ranged from flat landscapes to steep cliffs and rollicking canyons, its profile gradually changing as the shuttle crisscrossed on the concrete freeway. The outline of the Sea of Cortez was faint in the distance. It took hundreds of years and countless cycles of weather patterns for this unique topography to form. The giant saguaro grew, lived, and flourished in this time. For them, years pass like minutes, and decades last like hours. I respected the stillness of the desert, and unlike the sea, its slow resistance to change. *Sonora* implies sonority, which refers to resonance and loudness. I suppose it is a poetic name for a place filled with deafening silence.

The shuttle stopped at a small store on the roadside to take a short break. I spotted the stark black and white contrast of an osprey.

The seahawk surveilled the world below from atop a lamppost. Perhaps it was scanning for prey. Or perhaps it was observing hapless humans — clumsy, wingless creatures burdened by their inability to take flight.

Puerto Chale

I eventually reached Puerto Chale and hopped onto a speedboat. Fog hung heavy and low on the brackish water and coastal salt flats. But the boat cut through the thickness, its motor purring a steady reverberating hum.

Mangroves appeared, their trees clinging to the mud, roots cast horizontally like a wide net. Various species of birds coexisted on the banks. They shared the space, like a busy *piazza* where people congregate, minding their own affairs. The mangroves and inlets ultimately gave way to the open ocean — boundless and all-encompassing, meeting the sky on the horizon.

There may have been fifty boats that day, bobbing and zipping on the water. Some circled round with the hope of spotting a gray whale — perhaps even glimpse its spray or feel its touch. A hundred or more mature whales and calves surrounded the vessels. Most were bigger than the boats. Some turned on their sides and waved their fins. Some grew curious and approached the strange floating contraptions in the water. Some kept their distance, preferring to keep to themselves. One whale greeted me with a splash of cold water and a spray of cool mist.

The gray whales near Puerto Chale migrated from the Arctic to breed and raise their young in the winter months. The shallow lagoons and calm waters offered a safe, protected environment. Guided by instinct, they trusted the natural process and didn't fight it.

The whales' fins and bodies were covered by barnacles that had accumulated over time. The barnacles stuck to them even as they flipped, jumped, or thrashed in the cold water. I thought, perhaps that is what trauma is like to us humans. It stays with you throughout your lifetime, becoming part of who you are. It is said that the body keeps the score. We just learn to carry it and live with the things that weigh on us emotionally, mentally, and physically. The whales are outside our windows, but there exists a sea within us, with all that it contains.

The Ephemeral Nature of Whales

On the final day of my trip, I took a boat to a remote beach. It was surrounded by crystalline cyan waters and mysterious mushroom rock colonies. I dipped my feet in the shallows and touched a small fish. I showed the tour guide a video that I took of it, and she told me that it might have been a stonefish, which has a venomous sting.

I had lunch at Tres Virgenes, a Baja woodfire restaurant. The pear salad was like taking a bite of paradise. They also had red snapper and steak, which I was told were equally excellent. I randomly ventured into a bar that had a live band playing. Guitars and the room vibrated under the trio's dexterous fingertips, resonating with their dulcet tones.

Life becomes about appreciating the present moment and filling it with experiences — to create and preserve memories. We live our lives because we don't know what tomorrow will bring. Sing a little, dance a little, eat a little, drink a little tequila, and have a time worth remembering.

"Plato's view" is to look at things from above — stepping back, zooming out, and seeing life from a higher vantage point. It prompts us to gain perspective and remind ourselves how small we are in the grand scheme of things, and how small everything else is, for that matter.

What does matter if everything is ephemeral or temporary? The present matters. Plato's view teaches us to: Tap into the mutual interdependence with the whole of humanity. Take a step back from our own concerns and the worries of everyday life. Develop a global consciousness and mindset to do something about the state of the world we are living in.

Puerto Chale is a port brimming with wonder. Being there felt like living on borrowed time and space, a temporary visit to the world of whales. This haven was theirs. I was only lucky to get a glimpse of their natural habitat and migration journey. I wished I could rise up from that boat and see everything from an osprey's vantage point — to catch the silhouettes and shadows of whales as they surfaced and dove back into the ocean. Like all other things, whales are ephemeral and transient, only there for a season, when the right conditions aligned.

"Life can only be understood backwards; but it must be lived forwards."
– Søren Kierkegaard, Danish philosopher, father of existentialism

"It is the time you have wasted for your rose that makes your rose so important." – Antoine de Saint-Exupéry, The Little Prince

"Solitude sometimes is best society." – John Milton, Paradise Lost, Book IX, line 249

Part 2

Finance

Chapter 6

Money and Time (Low Risk/Reward)

Zen in Income Investing

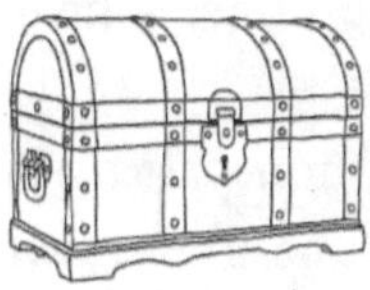

"The best day to invest was yesterday. The second-best day is today."

The Three States of Money

Money, as a social construct, takes many shapes and forms. Think of it like the three fundamental states of matter. Terms like liquidity, fluidity, and solvency reflect its changing nature. It ebbs and flows like a river. My mom, a banker, likes to tell me that's why money is called currency. Some have oceans, like the world's billionaires, most have ponds, while others have puddles.

Money is a solid tool. It is a means to an end, and not the end itself. You invest and follow a strategy to hone your money so that you can use it at some point in the future. You use that tool when you need to. That's what it's there for, after all. Then you'll make more money and hone it again, then you'll use it again when the need arises… and the cycle continues.

Money is elastic and compressible, like air. You can make it stretch or shrink. In hard economic conditions, it offers a measure of insulation. It is a conduit towards a better, more comfortable life. And it exists in the social (and digital) ether, with cash and credit cards being mere symbols. Like the concept of relationships, it is intangible. Our relationships are not only restricted to interpersonal ones. We must also consider our relationships with inanimate objects like food, exercise, alcohol, or money. In essence, we should be wise and spend less than what we make. This poses an important question: Do you have a healthy or unhealthy relationship with money?

Time, quite literally, is money. It has a temporal component and an exponential value over time. The snowball effect takes a long time to come into full force. However, the more you save and invest, the easier and faster your money will build and grow, like an avalanche.

Investing

At some point, everyone must ask themselves: In what ways can I make my money grow? Like the title of the 1995 comedy-romance "*While You Were Sleeping*" suggests, the path to wealth is to make your money work for you — while you are sleeping.

An investment is traditionally defined as the commitment of resources to something that is expected to gain value over time. Typically, the risk level of an investment is commensurate with its reward potential. However, this is not an inviolable rule. One's investment approach and strategy must reflect a multitude of considerations and contain a means of protection to be sound, strong, and sustainable.

These are some of the things I have learned from more than a decade of my own personal education in investing and finance.

High Yield Savings Accounts (HYSAs)

A type of savings account that offers significantly higher interest rates than traditional savings accounts. They allow your money to grow faster, often keeping pace with or beating inflation, though rates can change with market conditions. They are ideal for emergency funds and short-term goals, while remaining safe and liquid.

Shop for banks or credit unions that offer HYSAs, to ensure that your cash is never idle.

Certificates of Deposit (CDs)

A type of savings account that pays a fixed, agreed-upon interest rate on your deposit for a set amount of time, called the *term*. In return, the money must be left untouched in the account for the full duration of the term.

Research the special rates offered by different banks or credit unions to optimize your returns.

Treasuries

A debt security issued by a government (like the US Treasury) to raise funds. Types of Treasuries mainly differ by their maturity: T-Bills are short-term (under a year), paying interest at maturity, T-Notes are medium-term (two to ten years), paying semi-annual interest, and T-Bonds are long-term (twenty to thirty years), also paying semi-annual interest. These are sold at a small discount over the Treasuries' face value. Longer maturities typically offer higher yields (coupon rate) for the increased time commitment. All are considered very low risk due to government backing.

I opened a TreasuryDirect account so that I could purchase Treasuries from the government. This is generally safe because of the US dollar's status as the reserve currency. Because Treasuries are auctioned on a fixed schedule, you don't know the interest rate of the Treasury you purchased until after the fact. You have an indication based on the most recently auctioned Treasury, but it is not guaranteed. This is why it makes some sense to buy them in lots.

Treasuries offer an option to invest funds and earn interest while supporting one's personal goals (income, diversification, reasonable assurance of safety, stability, etc.) Gold is also seen as a safe harbor, along with other precious metals like silver. It is a commodity that has a history of behaving inverse to market performance.

CD (and Treasury) Ladder

A personal finance strategy for investing money across multiple CDs with staggered maturity dates, or Treasuries that pay interest semiannually or at maturity. The purpose is to balance interest earnings and access to funds.

Stagger the deployment of funds into CDs or Treasuries so that you can generate income for multiple months in a year. I did this so I could derive income from investments almost every month of the year.

The Economy and The Stock Market

Like the NASDAQ (National Association of Securities Dealers Automated Quotations), S&P (Standard & Poor's) 500, and DJIA (Dow Jones Industrial Average) composite indices, the Ten-year Treasury Yield is a key metric indicating the outlook for the future, and consequently the stock market's condition. In contrast, GDP (economic growth), unemployment, and inflation are key metrics that indicate economic health in the present and recently concluded past.

To me, the economy indicates the present, while the stock market indicates the future (based on investor confidence). This is my rudimentary understanding as to why the two are not synonymous or interchangeable. A method to reduce drawdowns in the stock market and shorten prolonged underwater periods is diversification — by holding uncorrelated assets like Treasuries, gold, and bonds.

Municipal Bonds

Financial instruments offered by local governments to raise money for public works projects.

Some years ago, I met Tony, who worked as a financial adviser at one of the "Big Four" US banks. He advised me to invest money in municipal bonds. They are relatively low-risk and provide regular fixed income. Investments serve different purposes. In this case, it served as an income investment rather than a growth investment.

Municipal bonds are a source of local government funding. It funds local government projects such as the construction of roads, bridges, buildings, schools, and water systems in different cities and states across America. In return, it pays the bondholder in interest.

Tony presented me with a prospectus that detailed these projects and locations. The complexity and interdependence of our multilayered society fascinated me. I learned a little about the functions and workings of government through municipal bonds. Like Treasuries, they are critical to the execution of government projects that rely on different sources of public funding.

Defining Risk

Risk tolerance is subjective and differs from person to person based on their personal circumstances and stages in life. What I present here is based on my own spectrum of risk from my own experiences — the wins, losses, and lessons. It is for you to assess how you define your own low, medium, and high-risk levels.

Balancing Liquidity with Long-Term Strategy

Part of my financial education has involved learning how to allocate assets as market conditions shift and interest rates change. There are times when CDs offer better rates than Treasuries, and times when Treasuries are more attractive than CDs. Financial institutions (banks, credit unions) also change their promotions based on their goals, strategies, or prompts from leadership. Sometimes, this bank would have higher rates than that bank, and other times, it would be the opposite. Being able to shift investments, optimize yields, and take advantage of better deals has a substantive impact on one's finances, which determines fiscal well-being and standard of living.

Like in the game of Monopoly, however, a person should never keep all their assets tied up in securities. Always keep cash on hand for emergencies and unexpected life events.

The stock market is said to transfer wealth from the impatient to the patient. It is naturally difficult in the winter of discontent. Imagine that you have been diligently investing for three years, enjoying watching your account grow and flourish. Then, a meltdown transpires. You lose not only three years of growth, but you now have less than when you originally started. Do you panic and sell? No. You must be mentally prepared to hold underwater and trust that growth will eventually return.

Like in *Game of Thrones*, a sweet summer child is one who is born and raised in a time of ease. But rest assured, winter (recession/depression) is coming.

Zen in Finance

When it comes to investing, I found that dispassionate and unemotional detachment leads to better investment decisions in the end. Yes, money can be a tool to achieve happiness, but it is never the source of it. Zen teaches us that greed leads to suffering. I find this philosophy applies to finance and investing as well.

Someone once asked me, "Well, what if the stock market crashes completely and never recovers?" I responded, "In the event that happens, there will be much bigger things to worry about than money."

Volatility is the nature of financial markets, so we ourselves must be centered. They exist outside of our control. What we can control are our own financial plans and investment strategies. If we are fiscally responsible, in time, we can grow our money in time from a tiny sapling to a mighty oak — one that can weather the long winter.

Chapter 7

Money and Time (Medium Risk/Reward)

Stoicism in Growth Investing

"Time in the market beats timing the market."

A Simple Strategy

For the diligent investor, conventional wisdom dictates adding to one's portfolio or contributing to one's brokerage account on a regular basis. Compared to income investments that are used for daily spending, growth investments serve a long-term purpose.

I admit that I am a large proponent of index funds and have cultivated them for more than a decade. The ultimate goal is to reach a certain amount by retirement age, at which point the accounts will ideally be self-sustaining. This is where compounding interest comes into play: money's potential for exponential growth.

The thirty-year average yield for the S&P 500 is 10 percent, given each year will be different and can vary widely. Your goal amount can be calculated based on the annual expenses you expect to incur at retirement age. The inflation rate is also an important factor to consider in your calculations. Once your investment reaches your goal amount, periodic withdrawals of 10 percent can be skimmed off the top every year for the remainder of your life, while the account continues to replenish itself. This is what generations of wise Americans have done. That is the working theory, anyway.

For example, say you have $1 million in an S&P 500 index fund. You can withdraw $100,000 a year, since the money will, *on average*, grow $100,000 a year. I assume a conservative average annual yield of 7 percent, which was the ten-year average in 2022. Because of the 2023-2025 three-year bull run, the ten-year average-to-date sits at 13 percent. Most funds also yield a quarterly dividend, the amount of which depends on the type of fund.

The Logic of Index Funds

An index fund is a type of mutual fund or exchange-traded fund (ETF) that passively tracks a market index, such as the S&P 500. It aims to match the performance of an index by investing in all the same securities (stocks, bonds, etc.) with similar weightings, offering a diversified and low-cost way to invest in the broader market.

Some categories of index funds include size-focused (small-cap, mid-cap, and large-cap), sector-focused (like green energy, technology, and REITs), and geography-based (like global, international, regional, developed, and emerging markets). The most popular are broad-market index funds, which track major composite indices like the NASDAQ (all three thousand + stocks listed on the stock exchange), S&P 500 (the leading five hundred companies listed on the stock exchange), and DJIA (thirty prominent companies listed on the stock exchange).

Stocks represent single units of ownership in a company that are traded in discrete quantities, often referred to as "lots". Each is listed at the cost amount at which you purchased them. But unlike stocks, an index fund is a pooled investment vehicle. It is listed at a single price, which reflects the average value of the entire basket of underlying securities. This means if you buy two units of stock at two different times, you will see two different lots with two different cost amounts. If you buy two units of an index fund at two different times, they will be pooled together, and you will see one average cost amount. This makes it an ideal vehicle for long-term investing.

Additionally, index funds are accessible to everyone. They do not require specialized knowledge, and you don't need to be an expert in quantitative analysis — the application of advanced mathematical/statistical/computational models, complex science and programming (like Python) used in analyzing financial markets, developing trading strategies, managing risk, and pricing securities. It's not rocket science. Boring investing is often good investing. For most, success in leverage or algorithmic trading are only chance occurrences and not viable strategies. But anyone can achieve success in investing. I don't purport to know any better. I simply try to learn from the values cultivated and taught by some successful investors.

Jack Bogle

Bogle's philosophy focuses on broad-market index funds, minimal fees, diversification, and staying the course through market ups and downs, rather than picking individual stocks or trying to time the market.

He founded Vanguard, a major US investment company with $11 trillion in global assets under management (AUM) as of 2025. It is known for low-cost mutual funds and ETFs.

A "Boglehead" is an investor who follows the simple, low-cost, long-term investment philosophy of Vanguard founder John C. (Jack) Bogle. They value financial simplicity, discipline, and the steady building of wealth over decades. (Bogleheads.org)

Warren Buffett

Buffett's philosophy is primarily centered on value investing and a long-term, patient approach. It emphasizes buying shares of high-quality, easily understandable businesses at a fair price, and holding them essentially forever.

He transformed Berkshire Hathaway, a failing textile mill, into a massive American multinational conglomerate with $1 trillion in total assets as of 2025. It owns numerous companies like GEICO, Duracell, Dairy Queen, Fruit of the Loom, and See's Candies.

Despite his immense wealth, Buffett is known for his modest habits and simple lifestyle, preferring hamburgers and Cherry Coke. A major philanthropist, he has pledged to give away virtually all his wealth through the Bill & Melinda Gates Foundation and his own initiatives. (CNN)

J.L. Collins

Collins's three core rules — spend less than you earn, invest any extra money in low-cost index funds, and avoid debt — offers a blueprint for financial growth. He is the international bestselling author of *The Simple Path to Wealth: Your Road Map to Financial Independence and a Rich, Free Life.*

The Financial Independence, Retire Early (FIRE) community has called him "The Godfather of FI". (Simon & Schuster)

The Length of Investment Horizon

Ultimately, an investment strategy should hinge on the length of one's investment horizon. As one gets closer to retirement age, it makes more sense to rebalance toward a more conservative portfolio that is weighted more heavily toward safer instruments like bonds.

For now, continue to make regularly timed additions, dollar-cost average and build. I held steady and tested my resolve by weathering some stormy markets: 2020, 2022, and the first half of 2025, as well as the flatline in 2015-2017, when I first started my investment journey. Over the years, I learned to make decisions with long-term considerations in mind, and not short-term wins.

Here's the catch: People sometimes die prematurely, develop severe health issues, or reach retirement age during a recession. You defer enjoying life only to die or become disabled before you can do it. And so, a balance must be struck somewhere between the two.

Stoicism in Finance

The two biggest emotions that come into play in investing are fear and greed. Stoicism helps manage and temper those emotions that can cause us to make impassioned, impulsive, and illogical decisions. This often takes the form of panic buying due to fear of missing out (FOMO) or panic selling driven by fear that the sky is falling. Truth be told, the finance industry makes far less money off passive investing with fewer management fees.

Listen closely, but respond accordingly. Disregard the noise and the fearmongering from outside. Practice temperance during the tempest, in times of *sturm und drang* (meaning storm and stress). Remaining focused on my long-term strategy is what helped me during the drawdowns over the years.

2020

No one is infallible, not even the experts. Tony, who was assigned as my financial adviser at my bank, instructed me to withdraw the funds I had invested in the S&P 500 in my self-managed brokerage account, and put those funds into municipal bonds in an account he managed. I could not believe what I was hearing. This was clearly an unserious person. I learned then and there, this is not someone to be trusted.

Tony wouldn't let me withdraw from the account he managed (and earned a commission on). He would ask why I wanted to withdraw those funds. Armed with his graphs, quants, and projections, he would convince me that he was right and I was wrong, and that he knew better than I ever could. After all, he had applied skills in calculus, probability, statistics, and programming to create his elegant algorithms.

Eventually, I told him I was going to use the funds as a downpayment for a house for my poor, sick grandparents. (A little white lie.) Well, he couldn't refuse. Like a petulant child, he begrudgingly closed the account. I did the opposite of what he told me, and I don't regret a thing. I am so thankful that I followed my internal compass. Personally, I learned that I am my own best financial adviser.

Looking back, I realize that Tony is an excellent salesperson but a questionable financial adviser. Even if he is a fiduciary, our interests were in conflict. He even attempted to use a market crash to further his own agenda. He was there to sell a product and make money for himself. Today, everyone I know who worked at that bank location has come and gone, except for Tony, who is still there. He is very, very good at his sales job.

It is important to note that everyone's experience is different. Jeff, a fellow investor, swears by his financial advisers and has found great success working with them. He has a different investment philosophy, which obviously works for him. There are different paths to financial success.

2022

The yearlong bear market was driven by peak inflation during the 2021–2023 surge and the resulting increases in interest rates. This was combined with the worst year for the bond market since 1994.

A global recession was feared to be on the horizon, due to a decline in economic indicators and an inverted yield curve. All this was exacerbated by supply chain disruptions due to the Russian invasion of Ukraine and uncertainty over the long-term effects of the COVID-19 pandemic on the economy.

But the market recovered and surged for the next few years. In hindsight, 2022 was a terrific opportunity to buy stocks, bonds, or mutual funds at a healthy discount.

The First Half of 2025

At times of great fear or uncertainty, it is natural to consider selling or rebalancing one's portfolio. I entertained the idea during the tariff uncertainty. *No, everything is different this time* was the popular sentiment, and everyone would list their litany of reasons. I contemplated whether it would serve me better to liquidate before the market sinks. I talked to people who exited their position in the middle of the downturn. They didn't get a chance to jump back in before the stock market rebounded in May.

It is always a gamble and a risk to time the market: You must be right not once, but twice — when to exit and when to reenter.

Another substantive consideration when you sell your portfolio all at once is that the action will trigger a taxable event. The gains you have made will be actualized in the year you liquidate or exit your position. Will your gains be offset by the income taxes you will then owe, which could be around a quarter of your profit? There are many factors to consider.

Future Industry Bubbles and Index Funds

Anything can happen. Some believe that artificial intelligence (AI) is a bubble that can pop at any moment, triggering a recession.

This would also affect certain index funds, as the S&P 500 is so heavily weighted toward AI companies such as Nvidia, which has a market cap of $4 trillion in 2025.

But remember that the S&P 500 index is not forever set in stone. It rebalances quarterly on the third Friday of March, June, September, and December. These regular adjustments maintain the index's accuracy by updating company weights and ensuring it reflects the US economy. As a result, the S&P 500 will always favor the leading and most prominent public companies. If Nvidia fails, for example, it will be dropped from the index, and a new company will take its place.

Of course, a falling tide sinks all ships. The broad market will be affected if AI's performance falls short of expectations. However, diversification in different industries can provide a modicum of safety.

Future Recessions and Dollar-Cost Averaging

No one knows what the future holds. The five-year period from 2007 to 2012 encompassed the "Great Recession" and its aftermath. This was marked by the collapse of the US housing bubble, the subprime mortgage crisis, and the global financial crisis — leading to stock market crashes, government bailouts, and massive job losses. A slow and uneven recovery extended well into the early 2010s, which was a time of increased regulation (Dodd-Frank Act) and lingering economic pain.

By committing to a long-term strategy and a steady habit, one can ride out recessions and still come out on top, even if it takes years, like the Great Recession. This is where dollar-cost averaging comes into play.

Dollar-Cost Averaging (DCA)

This is an investment strategy where you invest a fixed amount of money at regular intervals, regardless of the asset's price. The goal is to smooth out your average purchase cost over time and reduce the risk of buying at a market peak.

By consistently investing the same sum, you automatically buy more shares when prices are low and fewer shares when prices are high. This lowers your overall cost per share and minimizes the impact of market volatility, making it a great strategy for long-term wealth building without trying to time the market.

The Story of Sisyphus

In Greek mythology, Sisyphus is tasked to push a giant boulder up a hill for eternity. But every time he gets close to the top, it rolls back down.

The story of Sisyphus can be considered an allegory for the stock market. As markets rise, we feel powerful. But when there is a crash and our positions drop, we feel powerless. Months or years of progress can vanish in days or weeks. It feels hopeless to keep trying, but that is the nature of market cycles.

A market crash or recession is not a sign that we are doing something wrong. There is simply no end to the process of discipline and maintenance when it comes to investing. It is important to accept that markets move in cycles, drawdowns return, rebalancing requires prudence, and discipline beats prediction every time.

Market drops are inevitable, but so are rises. Long-term investors who accept the cyclical nature of the markets will always outperform those who chase shortcuts. Everyone's rock rolls back eventually, but the test is whether we continue to push.

Chapter 8

Money and Time (High Risk/Reward)

Jungian Psychology in Private Investing

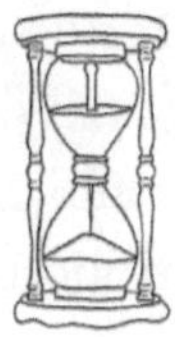

"Never risk something that you need for something that you want."

Private or Angel Investing

In this type of investing, an accredited investor provides capital for a business startup or early-stage company in exchange for ownership equity or convertible debt. In addition to funding, the investor can offer valuable mentorship and industry expertise. Angel investing carries higher risk and has the potential for higher returns compared to traditional investing, as it supports new companies that are often unproven.

Because such companies are not publicly traded on the stock exchange, they are considered secondary markets. The investment often provides a direct stake on the company's capitalization table. The investor sees a return on their investment if the private company becomes public or is acquired.

Note that a public company sells its shares to the public on a stock exchange. It is subject to rigorous SEC regulations and disclosure requirements. A private company, meanwhile, doesn't publicly trade its shares. It is instead held by a small group of owners/investors.

Asset Allocation

It is up to each individual to decide on the asset weight allocation that is appropriate for them, based on their own personal circumstances. The 70:20:10 portfolio allocation is an investment strategy where 70 percent of one's portfolio is allocated to low-risk investments, 20 percent to medium-risk investments, and 10 percent to high-risk investments. This can help manage future uncertainty and facilitate balanced growth. I maintain a similar allocation (65:30:5), with less than 5 percent in high-risk assets.

Private investments are at the high-risk end of my investment spectrum, with income investments at the low-risk, and growth investments in the middle. They are considered long-term investments for my legal business entity.

I used a very small fraction of my business profits to invest in pre-revenue and emerging companies that could potentially have national consequences and universal impact. The portion I allocated is attributed to disposable income. I would not suffer a considerable loss if any or all the investments collapsed.

Due Diligence

There are many companies out there. Like buying a business, one must conduct one's due diligence to determine whether a private company is viable, and more importantly, a good investment.

Compared to public companies, they are not as heavily regulated by the Securities and Exchange Commission (SEC).

My decision to invest in a private company is based on my own due diligence of the company, the founders, and the leadership team. Below is an informal checklist of my key conditions.

(1) Valuation: A quantitative process of determining the fair value of the investment. The company can generally be valued on an absolute basis (on its own) or on a relative basis (compared to other similar companies). To be an investible company, it must have favorable terms and comparables.

Valuation is paramount. Do you think it properly reflects its present value? Is the company overvalued or undervalued? And do you believe its future value will increase? The potential reward should be commensurate to the risk involved. Not all good businesses are investible businesses. There must be enough meat on the bone for the company's shareholders.

(2) Value Proposition: A clear and concise statement that communicates why a customer should choose a company's product or service over those of their competitors', highlighting both tangible and intangible benefits. The company must address a need in the market and how it can fill that gap (including Problem, Solution, Business model, Market, and Moat).

(3) Due Diligence Report: A comprehensive document prepared by an independent team, summarizing findings from a thorough investigation into the company. It is designed to verify information, ensure compliance and accountability, uncover hidden risks and liabilities, and support an informed investment decision.

This report offers a deep dive into the company's rationale, track record, and strategy. It provides an evidence-based view by analyzing financial/legal records, operational health, and commercial viability, and it acts as a risk-management tool before committing to a deal. The content and quality of the due diligence report are critical.

There must be a path to the finish line — all businesses encounter roadblocks, but they should be surmountable. The due diligence report shows how.

(4) Non-Dilutive Funding: Capital provided to businesses without requiring any company equity or ownership in return. Common forms include grants, loans (including venture debt or small business loans), prize money from competitions, tax credits, and vouchers.

Grant approvals from bodies like the National Institutes of Health (NIH) invoke trust and faith. It provides additional vetting from an impartial and verifiable source in the same field that may know more than you do.

(5) Management Team Funding: The commitment and funding of sizable amounts by management and board members convey their confidence, motivation, and optimism in the company and its mission.

(6) Purpose of Funding (and the ability to raise it): What are the reasons for the funding round? Funding fuels essential activities from initial setup (R&D, legal fees, working capital) to scaling (new equipment, inventory, staff) and provides a crucial financial safety net. It enables innovation, market expansion, and coverage of unexpected costs. Raising money must be in accordance with accomplishing actionable goals, not just to raise money for the sake of it.

The biggest risk for start-ups is running out of money, so the ability to raise it over a long period of time is imperative. When such an event occurs, they will be essentially dead in the water. Do you trust that the company's leadership team can sustain interest, deliver on their promises, and use your money wisely?

(7) Investing in the People: Just as important as the company itself is the team running it. The company's people are arguably its most valuable assets. Research their biographies, past achievements, and credentials. The team must be up to the task and capable of achieving the company's mission and goals.

For example, having a unicorn founder at the helm is a benefit. This could be seen as a positive indicator of the company's future success. (A unicorn founder is the leader of a privately held company valued at over $1 billion. It is a rare achievement, coined by Aileen Lee to signify mythical success. They are often visionaries, deeply committed, disruptive, passionate, and skilled at building teams.)

(8) Vetting from Other Investors and Groups: Invest time to obtain valuable feedback from existing investors and gauge interest from potential investors by meeting with them. Listen to what is *not* being said, as well as what is being said. What is the intention behind their words?

Investor groups have a formal process for companies seeking to pitch to their investors. This weeds out most, but not all, un-investable companies.

(9) Derisking of Assets: This means reducing exposure to potential loss. The alleviation, if not removal, of certain risks by a company is an important consideration for an investor. This can include multiple assets, warrants, or risk-sharing mechanisms.

(10) Soft Qualities: Qualities like consistency in words and actions, follow-through, and respect are indicators of a quality company. Much like in life, observe people's characteristics over a period of time, and never rush to make an impulsive decision.

(11) Tertiary sources: Google, social media, and independent sources are good ways to check for red flags. People will always put their best foot forward, and companies are the same. Verify, do not rely on first impressions, and never make an important decision while under duress.

(12) Timing: There is a sweet spot between being too early and being too late. It is ideal to come in just at the right time, on the cusp, when the investment is derisked enough, but the return on investment can be maximized in a desirable timeframe.

Private Investor Associations

As a company grows, the typical flow for funding is: Personal funds > loans from family and friends > angel and private investors > family offices > venture capital (VC) > initial public offering (IPO) or acquisition. Most small businesses stop and remain at the family and friends stage.

Start-ups require more funding than family, friends, banks, or the Small Business Administration (SBA) can loan them, because they require a long ramp-up period before they can generate revenue. In Seattle, private investor groups such as Alliance of Angels, Keiretsu Forum—Northwest Chapter, and the Seattle Angel Conference help connect startups seeking funding with private investors by facilitating deal flow. An advantage of joining one of these groups is that companies must undergo a rigorous and robust screening process (which includes multiple rounds) before they can present in front of investors.

Early-stage investor groups use deal management platforms like Dealum, a comprehensive suite of tools to manage the investor's pipeline and portfolio, from deal intake to evaluation to post-investment screening. The funnel for start-ups is as follows: Roadshow > Showcase > Due Diligence > Syndicating > Past Syndications.

In the deal room, the investor community has access to companies' materials, such as their one-pager or fact sheet, pitch deck, and due diligence reports. They also receive information on the key team members of the company.

If an investor and a company close a deal, the investment details are stored on digital platforms like Carta, an enterprise resource planning (ERP) system that offers investors with transparency and control across their equity, fund, and portfolio. It also includes cap table management, equity management, security issuance, and ownership tracking. The software digitizes stock certificates and provides tools for 409A valuation and compliance — an independent appraisal of a private company's common stock fair market value (FMV).

An informative resource on private investing is *The Intelligent Investor* by Alison Davies and Matthew C. Le Merle. It contains practical wisdom from fifty leading Silicon Valley angels and venture capitalists.

Startup Companies

I learned about more than a hundred companies through weekly deal screenings, forum meetings, deep-dive/breakout sessions, and annual expos. A select few met my criteria and ultimately closed deals.

The companies were headquartered in different states across the country: New Jersey, Arizona, Pennsylvania, and California. They operated in different fields, like pharmaceuticals, life sciences, and biotech. (Someone told me that meant I am industry agnostic.)

The first company is developing novel, nonaddictive, non-opioid treatment for neuropathic pain. The second is developing therapeutics for hypoxia in oncology, stroke, brain tumor, and other indications. The third is developing next-generation cancer immunotherapy using AI-driven spatial analytics.

The fourth is developing plasma-based excavation and tunneling systems for underground infrastructure. The minimum investment required for a direct line on their cap table was too high. However, they also raised capital on Netcapital and Wefunder — online crowdfunding platforms for investing in early-stage startups at an affordable cost in exchange for equity.

There were also companies I came close to investing in but ultimately did not, for various reasons: A sustainability-native brand that was fully digitized and circular. A distributed carbon-capture solution that helped buildings achieve decarbonization goals. A venture capital fund, which is a basket of private companies (compared to a mutual fund, which is a basket of public companies). I felt that the potential reward did not justify the risk involved for this VC fund, even if it was more diversified than a single direct investment.

Someone from the investor group once told me, "Investments are like trains. If you miss one, another one will always come along."

The Economic Ecosystem at Large

The health and stability of the economy play a significant part in a startup's success or failure. There are years when government inspires investor confidence. This translates to open pockets and funding, increasing the likelihood that these companies could reach a milestone, an inflection point, or a liquidity event. Then there are years when the economic environment becomes less than conducive, or even inhospitable. Government funding and investors' wallets contract, making it even more challenging for these companies to reach important thresholds and accomplish their mission. In anticipation of these times, most investors stockpile funds as dry powder and deploy cash when opportunity arises.

Because start-ups and emerging companies don't exist in a vacuum, there is no such thing as the perfect economic environment. This is why it's hard and businesses fail. It is each investor's job to perform their due diligence and decide, based on their own criteria, when the time is right for them.

The Long-Term Financial Outlook

Evaluate the worst-case and best-case scenarios. In the worst-case scenario, I won't lose my shirt due to the allocation size in high-risk investments, and my future won't be impacted.

In the best-case scenario, one or more of my investments will yield a return, which I would use to fund more investments spread out across multiple companies. An optimistic timeframe is five years from the time of investment. Ideally, I would see a return each year to clear a financial runway. As of the time of this writing, all companies are alive, kicking, and gaining traction a few years later.

A Conundrum Between Business and Investing

One of the features of the investor group was their "mindshare" meetings. A subgroup of the same ten people met once a month to discuss their prospective investments, give updates on their existing investments, and share their knowledge of investing.

Geo, my mindshare group's moderator, used to be a professional who worked in the tech industry in Redmond. After working for a large corporation, he thought about resigning to strike out on his own. He had saved a healthy sum of money to spend on his new venture. Two paths lay in front of him: One, use that money as working capital to start a small business. Two, use that money to invest in ten different start-ups as an angel investor. He argued that it was safer for him to do the latter. Doing so offered diversification. He trusted those who knew more than him and had more experience in their respective fields.

I can't speak to the veracity of his logic, but it is an interesting perspective worth considering. There are different paths to financial independence. The main drawback of this approach would be cashflow. It would take several years (if that) for an angel investment to make a return, whereas cashflow could be almost immediate in a small business. Another disadvantage is you hand over control once you hand over the check. You leave your destiny in someone else's hands, capable as they may be. Things can change.

Nothing is ever certain. Anything can and will happen — external factors that will affect a company either positively or negatively. External conditions are outside of one's control, like the wind affecting a sailboat in the ocean. The wind can be either against it, holding it back, or with it, propelling it forward.

Jungian Approach to Finance

A key concept of Jungian philosophy is the belief that each person has their own path to follow. By exploring the conscious and unconscious mind, one can uncover their true self and find meaning in life.

People invest in many different things, such as fine art, bitcoin, or Pokémon cards, because those are the things that resonate with them. I invested in businesses that resonated with me: those with causes that allowed me to contribute to society in a meaningful way.

It has been a rewarding experience to track the companies' progress from preclinical to clinical stage, from pre-revenue to revenue-generating phase. Patent approvals. First patient treatments.

I have seen them form partnerships in England, Scotland, Italy, Poland, Asia, and Australia. International collaboration is proof that we are still one world, and we can achieve great things when we work together. I take pride in knowing that I played a small part.

I was happy to invest in breakthrough technology that allows the building of underground power lines at a faster, more efficient and economic rate. This technology is long overdue in America. At the time of writing, heavy rains and winds in Washington caused the failure of several levee systems resulting in flooding and power outages from downed overhead lines. Sadly, power outages happen every year in my city due to strong winds. And sometimes, even due to small animals.

Since my investments are small and measured, I can use them to support businesses that aligned with my priorities and values. Money and time are precious resources requiring patience and restraint.

Chapter 9

Fifteenth Day of the Month

Routine, Ritual, and Rhythm of Financial Planning

A trail of ants flowed uninterrupted, like a river, under warm, gentle sunbeams. They made the best use of their time before the stormy weather, which would wash them away.

"The Ant and the Grasshopper" by Aesop (Jacobs version, 1894)

Originating from oral tradition, fables have been retold and rewritten across the centuries and generations. *Aesop's Fables* is a collection of short stories attributed to Aesop, an ancient Greek storyteller. These timeless tales convey virtues and vices to teach moral lessons about human behavior. Featuring talking animals, they have become foundational in the development and education of children across the world.

One such fable is about the importance of planning.

> *In a field one summer's day a grasshopper was hopping about, chirping and singing to its heart's content. An ant passed by,*

bearing along with great toil an ear of corn it was taking to the nest.
"Why not come and chat with me," said the grasshopper. "Instead of toiling and moiling in that way?"
"I am helping to lay up food for the winter," said the ant. "And recommend you do the same."
"Why bother about winter?", said the grasshopper. "We have got plenty of food at present."
But the ant went on its way and continued its toil. When the winter came, the grasshopper had no food, and found itself dying of hunger, while it saw the ants distributing everyday corn and grain from the stores they had collected in the summer. Then the grasshopper knew: It is best to prepare for the days of necessity.

The Moral

"The Ant and the Grasshopper" illustrates bookkeeping and budgeting by contrasting the ant's frugality, with the grasshopper's extravagance. While the ant works in summer to save for winter, the grasshopper plays all summer. This emphasizes diligence and planning to avoid hardship during scarcity in lean times. Present spending must account for future needs. This is in stark contrast with uncontrolled spending by living only for the moment.

This fable, going back to the sixth century BC, is a classic lesson in delayed gratification. It shows how foresight (bookkeeping/budgeting) ensures survival, while the lack of it leads to hunger and suffering. It highlights the importance of balancing work (earning/saving) and leisure (spending).

The Ant (The Bookkeeper and Budgeter): Works diligently, anticipates needs, accounts and sets aside resources from present abundance to cover future scarcity.

The Grasshopper (The Spender): Lives only for the moment, avoids consequences, and consumes all resources on immediate gratification.

The Summer (Financial Abundance): Represents when money is easy and time is plenty — health, wealth, income are high.

The Winter (Financial Hardship): Represents when income stops, but needs do not — times of uncertainty, unexpected expenses, sickness, job loss, retirement, old age.

The Moral (Budgeting Principle): A balanced budget isn't about deprivation. It's about resource allocation. It ensures the availability of reserves (savings/investments) so that "money works for you," rather than always working just to get by. It prioritizes future security over present wants.

Personal Finance as a Business

Human society collectively agreed to assign meaning to money. We believe in it in the same way we believe in other things like work, government, healthcare, insurance, taxes, culture, religion, and traditions.

Society also deemed money as a limited resource, which is what gives it value. Thus, each of us must make critical choices about what to prioritize and how, when, and where to allocate our resources. It is easy to lose track of one's expenses, so it is critical to live below one's means. And to live below one's means, one must first know what they have.

Bookkeeping is the process of recording a business's financial transactions. It ensures that financial reports are accurate and reliable. During and after my years working in small business, I learned to treat my personal finances as its own separate business and operate it as such. This meant doing my personal bookkeeping at least once a month, which usually landed on the fifteenth day. I monitored and measured my spending every couple of weeks or so, and I adjusted or controlled it if necessary.

Below I share some of the simple things that helped me declutter and organize the chaos, and in the process, take control of my personal finances and maintain financial composure.

Password Folder

Today's world requires us to have passwords and/or other unique security information (login name, account number, policy number, passcode, backup code, security questions, etc.) for each specific institution we use (bank, insurance company, utility company, HOA and mortgage, subscription service, retailer, etc.)

A password folder contains different passwords and other information, such as each institution's website and telephone number, all in one place. This information can be organized into categories. Mine include Financial, Personal, Volunteering, Wellness, Publishing, Retail, Social media, and Travel (mileage plan, rental car, city, etc.).

For recurring transactions or charges, I include the expected payment amount, frequency, and the day of the month each bank account or credit card will be charged.

This folder can also contain other vital information, like a person's passport number and social security number. Security protocols must be in place to ensure that the password folder is always safe, secure, and protected, since it contains sensitive information.

Frequency: Update as needed.

Financial Calendar

A financial calendar can track maturity dates of CDs, expiration dates of HYSA promotions, interest schedules for Treasuries, dividend payouts, due dates of bills/invoices, and/or due dates of tax payments. It is a helpful tool to keep track of important dates pertaining to one's personal finances.

I schedule all my bill payments to be "just on time", in the interest of cashflow. I also record payment information, including confirmation numbers, schedule dates, and payment dates.

Frequency: Update as needed.

Preparing Financial Statements

A monthly profit and loss (P&L) statement can include income by source and expenses by bank and category (including credit card bills, ATM withdrawals, HOA fees, electric bills, and others).

I determine my monthly net gain or loss after income and expenses. I account for any exceptional expenses that throw off "Actual" numbers. I observe the trends and compare them to "Last Year" and "Budget" numbers. Having the previous year's financial statements on hand helps me anticipate my upcoming expenses for the rest of the year, such as vehicle registration renewal (once a year), property insurance and tax payments (twice a year), and estimated tax voucher payments (quarterly).

Frequency: Every two weeks.

Maintaining Brokerage Accounts

I prepare a separate financial statement dedicated to my brokerage accounts, which is a different spreadsheet from the "Present" P&L. It includes information such as unrealized and realized gains (due to market price changes), taxable and nontaxable gains (from dividends, interest, and capital gains), and monthly interest.

Through the habit and discipline of bookkeeping, I can monitor the performance of my long-term brokerage accounts and compare the numbers to previous years. I make scheduled contributions to my brokerage account once or twice a month and contribute to my Roth IRA account until it is maxed out for the year.

Brokerage accounts typically only show total unrealized gains or losses. Maintaining a system to track them on a regular basis, recorded at the end of every month, regardless of deposits and withdrawals, is very helpful. I find that keeping a record and seeing past trends helps maintain my confidence during drawdowns, market crashes, and recessions. *Things in the present were never as bad as they seemed.*

Frequency: Every two weeks.

Reconciling Accounts

Reconciling bank and credit card accounts every month is a form of diligence and helps detect potential fraud. I keep all receipts, record all purchases without receipts, and track them against the corresponding credit card statements.

I like having just two credit cards — one for recurring transactions and one for everyday use. This helps to minimize the impact of potential card fraud. If the card I use for recurring payments is compromised, it would be a big pain to update the payment information for all my recurring bills (like auto insurance, health insurance, phone, cable & internet). If the "everyday" card gets hacked, it's just a matter of reporting and replacing it. Not having too many credit cards is more manageable and reduces the temptation to spend needlessly.

Frequency: Once a month.

Paying Bills

After reconciling my bank and credit card accounts, scheduling credit card payments and various other monthly obligations are the next priority. All my monthly bill statements were out by the fifteenth. Scheduling payments on the fifteenth day of the month allows me at least two weeks of lead time, as these bills are due on the first and eighth day of each month.

It is critical to pay all bills on time to prevent unnecessary late fees and penalty charges. Equally crucial is having enough cash in the bank to avoid overdraft fees. I used to have a personal line of credit, which I used to fund a small business. I have since repaid and closed the account.

Frequency: Once a month.

Folder > Filing Cabinet > Banker's Box

This is how I store physical data. (Yes, I admit that I am old school.) After reconciling my accounts and paying my bills, I put all receipts, statements, and other documents in a folder, which I store inside a filing cabinet. At the end of the calendar year, I move the folders to a storage or filing box (also called a banker's box).

I collect all the information needed for the annual tax organizer in a separate folder, along with all tax forms (1095-A, 1098,

1099, 5498) for the year. I use these to prepare my annual income tax return (1040), which is due every April. I note long-term capital gains, including equity held more than twelve months, as these have a lower tax rate.

It's not the most sophisticated system, but it works for me.

Frequency: Once a year.

Setting Budgets and Sticking to Them

Budgeting is the process of creating a plan to spend your money. The habit and discipline of budgeting will enable you to determine whether you have enough money to do the things you need or want.

An annual budget is created based on a person's ability to live on their generated income. Every month, I compare my actual spending to my budget, which is based on my expenditures from the previous year. Doing this influences my spending habits. My budget includes a buffer to accommodate any unexpected but necessary expenses (because life gets in the way). In line with this, I keep an emergency fund that is readily available for any unforeseen events or circumstances.

Frequency: Once a year.

A Philosophy to Live By

Observing these rituals and routines have allowed me to discover the simple joy of functioning in everyday life. In essence, financial planning is a gentle invitation to a more mindful and peaceful way of living, according to the steps of Zen philosophy:

Twelve Essential Rules of Zen Philosophy

1. Do one thing at a time: Practice single-tasking to maintain focus.
2. Do things slowly and deliberately: Move gently and thoughtfully through each action.
3. Complete what you start: Finish each task fully before moving on.
4. Do less: Eliminate unnecessary clutter.
5. Create space between tasks: Create breathing room for your mind to reset.
6. Build rituals: Small routines elevate daily moments.
7. Designate time to what matters: Prioritize what is important.
8. Devote time to sitting: Spend moments in silence and stillness.
9. Smile and serve others: Kindness and service are central to the philosophy.
10. Make "cleaning and cooking" meditation: Turn simple actions into mindful practices.
11. Reflect on what is essential: Find clarity by focusing on what matters.
12. Live lightly and simply: Cultivate peace by decluttering your life.

One Zen master in the eighth century said, "My miracle is drawing water and carrying wood." Today I say, "My miracle is bookkeeping and budgeting."

Chapter 10

Commerce or Scammers

Reflex, Reaction, and Response to External Forces

The world is rife with con artists, grifters, and hustlers who make it their life's mission to take advantage of the susceptible and the vulnerable. This has been happening since time immemorial.

The first scammer is often cited as Greek sea merchant Hegestratos, who, in 300 BC, attempted the earliest recorded financial fraud by trying to sink his own ship for an insurance payout. He planned to collect on a "bottomry" loan, which acted as a form of insurance policy on the vessel and its cargo. The agreement stipulated that the loan, plus interest, would be repaid upon successful delivery of the vessel's cargo. However, the loan would be forgiven if the ship were to be lost at sea. The merchant would be free of the debt, and the lender would lose the money. However, Hegestratos's plan backfired when his crew caught him, and he drowned while trying to escape.

Millennia later, scams have become increasingly prevalent in all aspects of modern society. It is my hope that this collection of stories will help you protect yourself from some of them by recognizing your reflexes, tempering your reactions, and responding more thoughtfully and deliberately.

The Long-Lost "Uncle"

One day, I received a letter in the mail at my business address. I read the envelope but didn't recognize the sender's name. It was from a barrister and solicitor who was a partner in a law firm in Ontario, Canada. I shall refer to him as "William Allen".

I present to you the content of William Allen's letter, for your perusal:

> *I am reaching out to you regarding a matter that may initially come as a surprise, as we have not previously communicated. Our firm is currently handling an unclaimed permanent life insurance policy belonging to our late client, Dr. Bruce Tiongson, a notable real estate developer and investor in Canada, who tragically passed away in an accident on Highway 400 near Barrie, Ontario, six years ago.*
>
> *The policy in question has accumulated a substantial amount of $10,550,300.00 USD deposited with a reputable bank. Despite our efforts, we have been unable to locate any of Dr. Bruce's relatives to claim this policy. According to the insurance company's policy regulations, unclaimed permanent insurance policies are to be surrendered to the state's abandoned property division after six years if no claim is made.*
>
> *Given the similarity between your last name and nationality with the deceased, I would like to propose a partnership with you to claim this policy. If you agree to this arrangement, I will facilitate the process of adding your name to the policy. In return, I would suggest a distribution plan where 10% of the funds will be*

> *allocated to charity organizations, and the remaining 90% will be divided between us.*
> *Please be assured that this process is entirely risk-free and handled with the utmost professionalism and confidentiality. I possess all necessary documentation to support the claim and expedite the process efficiently. It is important to note that the claim requires a high level of confidentiality and may take up to twenty business days from the receipt of your consent.*

As you can imagine, my gut reaction was ecstatic joy mixed with disbelief at my unbelievable good fortune. After the spike of euphoria had subsided, questions and suspicions started to swirl inside my head. I googled the barrister's name and credentials, and it turned out that he was a real, legitimate barrister and solicitor in Ontario. *This is very promising*, I thought.

I read his Google reviews. One person commented that the same thing had happened to him. He received a letter from William Allen, and he wanted to confirm whether the letter did in fact come from him. William Allen responded to the Google review and wrote that the letter did *not* come from him. He recommended the person report the letter to the authorities, and that he had done the same. Upon further inspection, I found that the real William Allen worked at a different law firm. William Allen was real, but the law firm seemed to have been made up by the imposter who sent the letter. The contact information was also not the real William Allen's.

The Publishing House or The Publishing Hoax

Out of the blue, I got a call from someone who worked at a publishing house — let's call it "Lawrence Publishing". The person I spoke with said that they had read my book and would like to offer me a publishing deal. They wanted to set up a time so I could meet with one of their literary agents.

After I hung up the phone, I researched Lawrence Publishing. It was a real publisher with a working website, physical address, contact information, customer reviews, and a list of published books and authors. It touted itself as "America's oldest publishing services company" with what seemed like a credible business model and practical tools for aspiring authors.

Delving deeper, I discovered some negative comments about their clients' experiences with the company. Apparently, the publishing house gets authors' information through the US Copyright Office. Lawrence Publishing then charges authors for their services, making a profit off the author rather than from selling the book.

This is what is known as a "vanity publisher" — a publisher that promises bestseller status but charges high upfront fees, lacks clear communication, or requires the author to buy their own books.

Another time, I got an email from someone named Ksenia. She claimed she was the organizer of a reading party on Meetup, a popular online event platform where people arrange meetups to share their interests. While Ksenia and the Meetup group were real, the person who sent me the email was an impersonator who asked for ridiculous amounts of money in exchange for being featured at a reading party. It was all a hoax.

As It Turns Out, You *Are* the Job

Any time you open yourself up to the world, you expose yourself to potential risk, liability, and scams. (This contrasted with when my life was more insular, and I just stayed in my protective bubble.) This even applies when you go out and apply for employment. During one of my job searches, I applied for jobs on job boards, aggregate sites, and company websites. I contacted recruiters, headhunters, and career centers. I came across job coaches (that charge $500 for their services) and courses (that cost $9,000).

An alarming number of companies turned out to be scams. Some clues: (1) When the company and job descriptions are vague and ambiguous. (2) When they don't say who their actual clients are. (3) When they make money off their employees instead of their customers. In the job market, these scams can manifest in the form of devil corporations, ghost jobs, and slave circles.

Devil Corporations

These are bait-and-switch companies that promise a fast track to an executive-level career in a fast-paced environment. Jobs are characterized by long hours, low commission, and a culture of pressure and intimidation. Employee salaries are presented as an incentive but are only attainable by a small group of executives who take a share of the sales. This leaves desperate people in even worse circumstances.

I experienced this when I applied to a Fortune 500 financial services company. The job listing they advertised was for a financial adviser role, but they were basically recruiting for a sales job in life insurance. I read about other people's experiences with the same company. It turned out to be a hard sales job.

Part of the hiring process entails giving them at least fifty of your personal contacts. You will then need to call your family and friends to sell them a life insurance policy. And if you leave the company, they get to keep your contacts. They will then have another employee contact your family and friends under the guise of knowing them through you.

"Hello, Aunt Evelyn? I know, it has been a long time since we last talked. How are the kids? Uh-huh. Wow, you must be so proud!... What? Oh no, I'm sorry to hear that. Life can be unpredictable sometimes... which is why everyone needs life insurance. Do you have one, by the way?" I could not see myself doing this and decided it was not for me.

Ghost Jobs

These are job postings that are intentionally misleading, either because the position doesn't exist or is not actively open for filling. These "jobs" are advertised to collect data, boost the company's reputation by creating the impression of a robust hiring process, or build a list of potential candidates to draw from when they do need to fill a position.

Most job listings on the internet are for ghost jobs, which is incredibly frustrating. You spend so much time and energy filling in long application forms and crafting cover letters specifically tailored to the jobs you are applying for, and it's all for nothing.

Slave Circles

These are direct sales/marketing jobs that share the characteristics of a pyramid scheme. They target vulnerable recruits, condition them, and use psychological pressure to make them conform to the company's mindset. There is usually a gap between what is communicated to applicants during recruitment and the reality of the day-to-day work.

There are some success stories, but employee turnover is high. These companies make money off their employees rather than their customers. To make money in this business model, they must attract people and make them stay in their jobs, regardless of the amount of money that they make. They sell employees a dream. But ultimately, they take advantage of people through empty promises of personal success and financial independence.

In my experience, most of these are sales/marketing companies with nondescript names like "Inspire", "Pinnacle Solutions", or "Limitless Promotions". They tend to contact you even if you never applied to them.

The Free Trip to Vegas or Southern California

Last summer, I went to a fair, where I came across a booth that was hosting a raffle. They asked passersby to enter their contact details into an iPad for a chance to win prizes. After a few months, I randomly received a phone call saying that I had been selected for an all-expenses-paid trip for two to either Vegas or Southern California.

Then came the catch. The woman on the phone was calling from a timeshare company. To claim the prize, I had to go to one of their offices and attend a ninety-minute presentation with the person I would be taking on the trip. Their nearest offices were in Tukwila and Vancouver. They employed the "act now" strategy: If we could be at their office at 6 p.m. on that same day, they would throw in meal vouchers. And if we could get there at 3 p.m., they would even throw in tickets to either Disneyland in Southern California or Cirque du Soleil in Vegas.

I didn't end up going. Everyone I talked to was familiar with the phrase, "free trip to Vegas or Southern California." They knew immediately. Apparently, timeshare companies have been employing the same sales strategy for the last thirty years or so. They use extremely aggressive sales tactics in their sales presentations, and they won't let you leave their office without buying a timeshare. I didn't want to put myself through that. The free trip would come with various catches and conditions, and the costs would most likely outweigh the benefits.

Be careful when you give away your personal information at fairs, festivals, events, or raffles. They often collect your personal information, which they can then sell to other companies. Here is some helpful advice on how to spot scams and protect oneself.

Tips To Spot Scams

Pretends to be someone you know

Scammers often pretend to contact you from agencies (like the Internal Revenue Service or Social Security Administration) or companies you're familiar with (like your bank). They might make up a name that sounds official or say they're contacting you on behalf of a loved one.

Presents you with a conditional prize or problem

Scammers may say you've won a prize that's too good to be true, and you must pay a fee to receive it. They might say you're in trouble with the government, or a family member is in trouble and needs money.

Pressures you to act immediately

Scammers want you to act before you have time to think. They might say your computer has a virus or a friend has an emergency. Sometimes they threaten to take legal action, arrest you, or freeze your bank account.

Asks you to pay in a specific manner

Scammers will often insist that you pay via wire transfer, a payment app, or by putting money on a gift card and then reading them the number on the back. Some will send you a fake check, instruct you to deposit it, and then ask you to send them the money.

Actions To Protect Yourself from Scams

Block – Filter and report unwanted emails, and block unwanted calls and texts.

Pause – If anyone says you must act right now, stop and ask yourself, "Is this how a legitimate company would act?" If something seems off, it probably is.

Refuse – Even if it's a person or business you recognize, don't give your personal or financial information to anyone who contacts you.

Resist – Don't let anyone pressure or threaten you into giving them money. Hang up or don't respond.

Validate – Instead of clicking links in emails and text messages, or calling the numbers provided to you, use a company's verified contact information from their official website.

Talk – If someone tells you to keep a secret or says something suspicious that makes you uncomfortable, stop and do a gut check with someone you trust.

(Chase Bank, chase.com/Fraudawareness)

Psychology of Scammers

According to the Federal Trade Commission, financial scams are on the rise, and no one is immune. In 2024, US consumers reported over $12.5 billion in fraud losses, a 25 percent increase from the previous year. Scammers are becoming more sophisticated, often targeting people during emotionally vulnerable moments, using pressure and secrecy to manipulate them. (Federal Trade Commission)

For all its faults, Google can be your friend. When in doubt, verify the company you are interacting with by looking into other people's experiences with them. More likely than not, you won't be the first person to have had this experience with them. I have spotted many a scam through finding what other people had to say about them — William Allen, Lawrence Publishing, the reading party, the timeshare company, and the various suspect employers I encountered in my job search.

When a computer is not connected to a local or public network, it is usually secure. However, when it is, it can easily be exposed to and infected with viruses and malware. It is the same with scams — they can reach us through mail, email, phone, or simply when we are out in the world. That is why it is imperative to be vigilant and put up literal and metaphoric firewalls:

Scammers do not target our intelligence, but rather trigger our emotions, such as fear, greed, loneliness, stress, sympathy, or anxiety from financial hardship. When we are in a highly emotional state, we bypass logical thinking and get forced into making hasty decisions. Individuals who can regulate their emotions under pressure are less vulnerable to persuasion.

Part 3

The Person

Chapter 11

Who Looks Inside

An Introspection

It is human nature to yearn for what is beyond our grasp. We dream of escaping to someplace far away, full of hope and optimism. We think we have not attained happiness because it lies elsewhere. Perhaps it can be unearthed in a different city, or even a distant country or continent.

Discussion Group

I once attended a discussion group where everyone in the room would nominate a topic, and the topics that received the most votes would be opened for discussion. Two or three topics would get picked. There were light topics such as your favorite book, favorite Christmas movie, happiest childhood memory, hidden talents, hobbies and pastimes, first concert, most recent travel destination, etc.

There were also serious topics: Making and keeping friends as you get older. Feelings of alienation or isolation. Disappointments and regrets. Health problems. Death. The state of funding for life-saving non-profits. The state of public transportation in the city. Human rights and ideological differences. The future of the country and the world. What scares or worries you? Who is your support group?

One week, the topic of migration was up for discussion. The questions were: Do you want to move to a different country? If so, which country would you move to? Each person shared their opinions and thoughts.

One person was in the process of making plans to move to Costa Rica. Another was in the beginning stages of claiming Irish citizenship by descent. Another used to work in China and wanted to go back. But there were also those who would choose to stay. Some contemplated the difficulties of losing their networks and support systems, starting over again, and finding belonging in a new community. One had to consider their medical condition, which was unlikely to be covered by the healthcare system in a foreign country. Another was a patriot who would live and die in this land.

Finally, it was the group facilitator's turn to speak. He was an introspective person with a unique perspective and deep insight into any topic of conversation. He talked about a concept called "geographic fix", describing it as a phenomenon where people think that their problems can only be solved by moving somewhere else.

Geographic Fix

Popularly used in Alcoholics Anonymous, geographic fix is the idea that moving to a new location can solve one's issues and quandaries, such as addiction or unhappiness. It is an attempt to solve an internal problem with an external solution, which is why it often leads to disappointment. Our geography is external. While moving to a new place can offer a fresh start, it is usually only a temporary reprieve.

If the problems you are facing and the challenges you are trying to escape are internal, you will take them with you wherever you go. Internal issues can only be addressed by making an internal change.

Of course, there are cases when moving to a new and different place can alleviate the problem you are facing. A common example would be moving from an expensive city with a high cost of living to a suburb with more affordable housing and necessities such as food, gas, and utilities. In this example, money, which is the external problem in question, is effectively alleviated by an external solution.

In the Movies

Movies have long expressed the concept of geographic fix through their storytelling. In *Under the Tuscan Sun*, the American protagonist buys a run-down manor in the Italian countryside following the deterioration of her relationship, a contentious divorce, and the dissolution of her marriage. But her problems cannot be solved by simply moving to a different country. She engages in a long, continuous process of evaluating her belief systems and reassessing her core values. After all, good and bad moments persist throughout our lives, no matter where we go. The answers to her problems do not come in the form she expects. Instead, it is her acceptance of impermanence and understanding of the temporary nature of life that frees her.

In *The Secret Life of Walter Mitty*, the protagonist embarks on a courageous mission to retrieve a missing photograph negative for *Life* magazine. His quest takes him around the world, to the farthest reaches of Iceland and the Himalayas, in search of meaning. Negative #25 literally captures the "quintessence of life," according to its reclusive photographer. The title character finds meaning not in the external world but by making an internal change — By living life to the fullest, exploring his passion, and pursuing experiences outside his comfort zone. It is being true and trusting himself that changes his life.

In *The Best Exotic Marigold Hotel*, a group of retirees travel from England to India, while in *The Hundred-Foot Journey*, a family of chefs travel from India to France, all in search of better lives. Two different movies that traverse continents and oceans, moving in the opposite direction, but with the same message: The most important journey you will take is the one inside yourself.

Inner Turmoil

Our decisions today are built upon our decisions of yesterday. When we are children, our options are narrow. We don't need to contend with challenging, life-changing questions. But as we get older and our world expands, we tend to experience a kind of vertigo. We get overwhelmed by the seemingly infinite options that are out there. Which direction is the right one for me? Am I making a big mistake? What is the point of it all?

And as we get even older, every decision seems to contract again. Each time we make a pivotal decision, we close other doors and eliminate alternative possibilities. Just thinking about this can lead to indecisiveness and analysis paralysis.

We can only make decisions based on the data that is available to us at any given time. We must give ourselves grace because hindsight is 20/20. It is a gift we receive only after a decision and its consequences have played out, not before.

In his book *The Body Keeps the Score: Brain, Mind, and Body in the Healing of Trauma*, Dr. Bessel van der Kolk, a pioneering researcher on traumatic stress, writes that our bodies store trauma, even if we are not aware of it. We must not confuse anxiety with attachment, and healing is a continuous work in progress.

How do you regulate your emotions? I did small things like breathwork, volunteering, participating in special-interest groups, playing board games, journaling, walking, and being outside in nature. I attended Mass at Our Lady of the Rosary, a sanctuary of serenity. There, I breathed in the comforting scents of frankincense and myrrh that drifted in the air. Doing these things helped get me out of my head and into my body.

Who Looks at Art

Art is a mirror, and it reflects what we see in ourselves. One of my favorite pieces is *Adrift* by James Jean, a contemporary Taiwanese-American visual artist known for his surreal style, intricate detail, and blend of Asian and Western influences. When I look at it, I see life as being adrift: It is chaotic and turbulent, but it is also a colorful and sonorous adventure.

In the past year, I have gravitated to the work of American photographer Gregory Crewdson. His art embodies the maxim "comfort the disturbed and disturb the comfortable". I must be one or the other, or both. His photographs capture ordinary moments, but there is something about them that feels "off". A curtain of separation called isolation hangs between his subjects and their surroundings. A quiet scream in a still photograph.

Hillary Weston, a staff writer for the Criterion Collection, says his work "creates a psychological space that allows viewers to create their own narrative. Two people can look at the same photo but tell themselves a completely different story." For more than two decades, photographer Gregory Crewdson has been creating otherworldly images that reveal an eerie side of Americana. His works, typically tableaux of small-town life, transform the everyday into the uncanny via a unique pairing of detachment and intimacy. (The Criterion Collection)

To me, the most resonant of films are the ones that reflect the human condition — the universal experiences, fundamental emotions, and existential questions that define human life. Rage in Martin McDonagh's fraught conflict set in rural America, *Three Billboards Outside Ebbing, Missouri*. Regret in Sam Mendes's pensive tale set in 1930s urban Chicago, *Road to Perdition*. Repression in Todd Haynes's examination of social norms set in 1950s suburban Connecticut, *Far from Heaven*. Resentment in Bong Joon Ho's commentary of late-stage capitalism in *Parasite*.

Desperation in *No Other Choice* by Park Chan-Wook. Grief in *The Farewell* by Lulu Wang. Trauma in *Midsommar* by Ari Aster. Loneliness in *Marty* (1955), directed by Delbert Mann and brilliantly acted by Ernest Borgnine.

Jungian Psychology

Carl Jung was a Swiss psychiatrist and psychoanalyst who founded analytical psychology to better understand human behavior and the psyche. He proposed that understanding one's own story brings freedom, and that the act of telling it within a safe space allows the mind to integrate it. The act of naming one's past creates coherence, and coherence paves the way for healing.

Psychology is not about ruminating or reliving the past. It is about understanding it. It is about placing each moment within a bigger picture, so the burden no longer lives inside your body. According to American psychiatrist Bruce D. Perry, "When you understand what happened to you, everything shifts. You begin to speak to yourself with kindness. You forgive the younger version of yourself. And you open the possibility of a different future."

Jung advocated for daily rituals in our everyday lives. Ritual could simply mean the rhythm of daily routine, the love for silence, or the habit of journaling. Because when we give our body rhythm, movement, and rest, we create space for peace. And in that space, the mind can begin to heal and feel at home.

Introspection

> *"Who looks outside, dreams. Who looks inside, awakes."* – Carl Jung

Jung suggested that the answers we seek are not in the external world but within ourselves. Dreams may inspire, but clarity comes from self-reflection. When we take the time to explore our hearts and minds, we discover who we truly are and what drive us: Becoming better as a person must be the most important project in one's life.

Self-discovery is complex. It challenges us to look inward, confront our unconscious, and take stock of the parts of ourselves we often ignore. However, these challenges are necessary to move forward and achieve a deeper understanding of ourselves.

Personal growth is rarely comfortable. Confronting the unconscious mind and embracing self-awareness often involve struggle and pain. But in this way, we can rise from our challenges, understand our motivations, and realize our authentic selves. According to Carl Jung, growth is a process of transformation.

Life ever flowing, ever changing, in Little Italy.

Chapter 12

The Dragonfly

Self-Realization in Change

Much of life is spent waiting. Waiting inside cars. Waiting in airports, restaurants, checkout lines, doctor's offices, hospital hallways. Waiting to take a bus or catch a cab. Waiting for a meeting to start, or a class or shift to end.

Change

> *"Trees don't 'lose' their leaves. They intentionally release them, knowing that by letting go, they ensure that the cycle of life continues. Beginnings are endings. Endings are beginnings… and that's all I've got to say about that."* – Sandie Ledray

Our view of the future shortens as we get older. Things become more immediate and urgent. The fleeting nature of life and the rapid passage of time become more pronounced. I don't know if it is because of the times we are living in or the general state of the world, but change seems to be occurring at an exponential rate and, at breakneck speed. It seems increasingly difficult to adapt when change is the status quo. I suppose that is how it has always been.

I talked to some people and listened to their counsel. Keri advised me to spend this time with family, if I am in the position to do so. I looked to different schools of philosophy for wisdom. I read different theories for guidance, from different parts of the world and eras in human history. However, they shared common concepts, applicable to different aspects of human life and society. Philosophy is the collective wisdom of our society's past, and it presents knowledge for understanding change. At some point in our lives, I believe we all ask ourselves, "What is it all about?"

The Shadow and the Self

To answer that question, we must venture somewhere that is hidden from us: The "Shadow" archetype represents the unconscious aspect of the Self. It contains the repressed emotions, desires, and aspects of one's personality that are considered unacceptable or undesirable by society. "Self", on the other hand, is the archetype representing the unified conscious and unconscious mind. It is the center of personality.

Deep-seated change is essential to become aware of the Shadow, integrate it into conscious awareness, and achieve wholeness. This involves confronting one's flaws and imperfections and accepting them as part of the Self.

Self-Realization

Life's purpose is to discover and fulfill our individual potential. Psychologist Carl Jung referred to this process as self-realization. Each person has a unique path to follow. By exploring our unconscious mind, we can uncover our true selves and thus find meaning in life.

For example, a person might have a passion for art. However, they never pursued it because they were told it was not a practical career choice. By exploring the unconscious mind, they may realize their true passion and understand that the pursuit of art is essential to their personal fulfillment. By following this path of creativity and self-expression, they may find meaning in life. (Anna Yusim, MD)

Dragonfly

Change is required for self-realization to take place. Nothing exemplifies this concept as eloquently as the dragonfly. In different cultures, dragonflies are seen as messengers of change and guides to new beginnings. Throughout its life, the dragonfly changes form — from aquatic nymphs below still waters to airborne adults with iridescent wings. This transformation represents becoming your true Self through adaptability, dynamism and the constant motion of change.

The agile dragonfly gently lands on the serene lotus flower, a picture of tranquility. It is resilient in different weather conditions and able to navigate complex environments. It shifts direction in midair, swift and nimble. It flutters across the water, rain, and air, seeking to discover what lies beyond the surface.

The dragonfly symbolizes self-realization, depth of character, and transformation — the kind of change that has its source in mental and emotional maturity, personal growth, and understanding of the deeper meaning of life. (Dragonfly.org)

Symbolism

Symbols can carry many meanings for different people. Throughout history, dragonflies have been interpreted in various ways, often reflecting our human nature and the virtues we value. In Japan, for example — sometimes poetically called *Akitsushima*, or Dragonfly Island — they were embraced by samurai as symbols of courage and strength.

In China, they symbolize good luck, harmony, prosperity, summer, and renewal. For the Hopi, Navajo, and Zuni tribes, purity, swiftness, healing, transformation, and connection to their crops. Celtic lore connects dragonflies to magic and truth, seeing beyond illusions, with some myths depicting them as fairies or dragons in disguise.

In some places in Europe, dragonflies are called darning needles, devil's familiars, ear cutters, or horse stingers. They are sometimes believed to be soul stealers that sew shut the mouths of liars and weigh the balance of souls. The Welsh name, *Gwas-y-Neidr*, means adder's servant and, reflects the belief that dragonflies follow snakes and even stitch their wounds. (LearnAboutNature.com)

Water Bugs and Dragonflies

In *Water Bugs and Dragonflies: Explaining Death to Young Children* by Doris Stickney, dragonflies symbolize the transition from life's waiting stage to its final transformation — death. Doris Stickney and her minister husband were searching for a meaningful way to explain the death of a five-year-old child to members of their community. While they were preparing for the memorial service, the fable of the water bug that changed into a dragonfly came to mind.

Near the end of her own life, Stickney first published this story in "Death," an article in the magazine *Colloquy* (December 1970).

It was then revised and expanded in 1982 to become the book *Water Bugs and Dragonflies: Explaining Death to Young Children*, which has been read around the world.

> *Down below the surface of a quiet pond lived a little colony of water bugs. They were a happy colony, living far away from the sun. For many months they were very busy, scurrying over the soft mud on the bottom of the pond. They did notice that every once in a while, one of their colony seemed to lose interest in going about with its friends. Clinging to the stem of a pond lily, it gradually moved out of sight and was seen no more.*
>
> *"Look," said one of the water bugs to another. "One of our colony is climbing the lily stalk. Where do you suppose he is going?" Up, up, up it went slowly. Even as they watched, the water bug disappeared from sight. Its friends watched and waited but it didn't return. "That's funny!" said one water bug to another. "Wasn't he happy here?" asked a second water bug. "Where do you suppose he went?" wondered a third. No one had an answer. They were greatly puzzled. Finally, one of the water bugs, a leader in the colony, gathered its friends together. "I have an idea. The next one of us who climbs up the lily stalk must promise to come back and tell us where he went and why." "We promise," they said solemnly.*
>
> *One spring day, not long after, the very water bug who had suggested the plan found himself climbing up the lily stalk. Up, up, up he went. Before he knew what was happening, he had broken through the surface of the water and fallen onto a broad, green lily pad above. When he awoke, he looked about with surprise. He couldn't believe what he saw. A startling change had come to his old body. His movement revealed four silver wings and a long tail. Even as he struggled, he felt an impulse to move his wings. The warmth of the sun soon dried the moisture from the new body. He moved his wings again and suddenly found*

himself up above the water. He had become a dragonfly. Swooping and dipping in great curves, he flew through the air. He felt exhilarated in the new atmosphere.

By and by, the new dragonfly landed happily on a lily pad to rest. It was then that he chanced to look below to the bottom of the pond. Why, he was right above his old friends the water bugs. There they were, scurrying about, just as he had been doing some time before. Then the dragonfly remembered the promise: The next one of us who climbs up the lily stalk will come back and tell where he went and why. Without thinking, the dragonfly darted down. Suddenly he hit the surface of the water and bounced away. Now that he was a dragonfly, he could no longer go into the water.

"I can't return," he said in dismay. "At least I tried, but I can't keep my promise. Even if I could go back, none of the water bugs would know me in my new body. I guess I'll just have to wait until they become dragonflies too. Then they will understand what happened to me, and where I went." And the dragonfly flew off happily into its wonderful new world of sun and air.

Change and Transformation

Much of life is spent waiting. Waiting inside cars. Waiting in airports, restaurants, checkout lines, doctor's offices, hospital hallways. Waiting to take a bus or catch a cab. Waiting for a meeting to start, or a class or shift to end.

Waiting to hear from an accountant or attorney. Waiting for a deal to close (or not). Waiting for a visa to be approved (or denied). Waiting for the current stage of life to end. Waiting for the next stage of life to start. A nymph, also called an immature, can spend five years of its life waiting before changing into a dragonfly. It will fly for a small fraction of its life, spending only a few months in its final form.

The adult dragonfly embodies a life fully realized. It symbolizes living in the moment and exemplifies living to the fullest, only achieved by integrating the Shadow into the Self. In this way, you are aware of who you are and what you want. And like the dragonfly, you can live your life without regret.

—

Dedicated to Sandie, who charted her own course, cast kindness in the places she went, and created the beauty she saw in the world.

Guitar with a maple leaf motif on the rosette and fretboard, made by Sandie Ledray.

Chapter 13

Good Luck Reunion

Individuation During Midlife

Ennui is a new friend in my life, and we have been getting to know each other. It has been my prevailing emotion as of late — a general feeling of malaise, of being stuck and rudderless, a sense of "been there, done that." This is not atypical for someone in their forties, I suppose.

The Reunion

I stepped through the gilded doors of the restaurant and informed the greeter that I was meeting a group of people. She enthusiastically herded me to a banquet table at the far end of the grand hall. I was the first one there, so I sat facing the door. The space was ornately adorned in the style of the Qing Dynasty, with vibrant colors, lotus motifs, and crimson-pink walls. Intricate latticework was etched into the ceilings, evoking a time of luxury and opulence. In a different time and place, Emperor Qianlong might have been seated in the center of the room, surrounded by his favored guests gathered for a festive and celebratory feast.

Near where I was seated was a seven-string *guqin*, the scholar's zither used for contemplation. It is a revered, quiet instrument played for personal cultivation, associated with morality, wisdom, and Confucian ideals.

One by one, my classmates from high school slowly trickled in, some of them with their spouses and children. It had been twenty-three years since we graduated together. What happened to all that time? I still felt the same as I did back then, sitting there with them in the room. Perhaps that is why we hesitate to see people from our past. Because in seeing the years etched across their faces, we are confronted with how much time has passed. We avoided talking about the past. Perhaps it was some kind of mass-induced denial. Instead, we talked about the present.

Morris and Miguel are successful entrepreneurs. They run multiple businesses and locations between them, creating and providing jobs to hundreds of people. Stanley is an executive at a large multinational. He lives and works in Australia. Ryan is a content creator with 200,000 subscribers on YouTube. He influences the culture and enjoys success as a public figure. Patrick is an advocate for the environment and sustainability. He works at the World Wildlife Fund (WWF) and is doing good for the world. Louie is a family man. He is a doting husband and a proud father to two small boys.

Louie's older son asked me for tips on writing. I told the nine-year-old, write about the things you like, whether that is school or Roblox. Write about what you are experiencing and what you are feeling, whether good or bad. In that way, you develop a habit of writing.

Jung's Stages of Life

And so, I took my own advice. I am writing about what I am experiencing and feeling today. Midlife is commonly the stage in life when one reassesses the steps they have taken, how they view themselves now in relation to childhood and adolescence, and how their present reality compares with their past expectations.

Carl Jung, the founder of analytical psychology, described human life as a developmental progression, unfolding in two distinct stages characterized by changing mindsets and priorities: the first half of life (childhood to middle age) and the second half (middle age to old age). According to Jung, the first half emphasizes outward development and the establishment of a persona, while the second half focuses on inward exploration and the process of individuation.

First Half of Life

Childhood: A period of development, of identity and sense of self, largely influenced by family and early experiences.

Youth: A period of exploration outside of the home and entering young adulthood. Characterized by a focus on physical appearance, athletic prowess, and proving oneself through competition.

Young Adulthood: A period of significant outward development driven by a desire to conquer and excel. Focused on building a career, establishing a family, striving to be the best in one's chosen field, and defining one's place in the world.

Second Half of Life

Middle Age: A time of transition when individuals often re-evaluate their life choices and past experiences. This stage involves turning inward, with a shift toward a more reflective and altruistic mindset, seeking meaning and purpose beyond personal achievement.

Old Age: A period when individuals often focus on their legacy, wisdom, and spirituality. This stage involves accepting mortality and seeking transcendence.

Jung believed that the second half of life comprises specific developmental tasks, just like the first half. While the developmental tasks for youth involve engaging in life and receiving external validation, the goal for the mature individual is the consolidation of a unified personality and inner growth. This is achieved by integrating the conscious and unconscious parts of their Self. "The first half of life is devoted to forming a healthy ego; the second half is going inward and letting go of it."

Afterlife: Jung also came to believe that life is but a segment of existence. "What happens after death is so unspeakably glorious that our imagination and our feelings do not suffice to form even an approximate conception of it."

(The Society of Analytical Psychology, thesap.org.uk)

Midlife

"Life really does begin at forty. Up until then, you are just doing research." – Carl Jung

To most, midlife is a wake-up call, and for many, it can lead to drastic action — by venturing into unknown territories in unexplored directions. A person's biggest mistakes can be made during midlife, but so can choices that will lead to their greatest successes.

It is the period from forty to sixty when a person often evaluates their own life. In the Jungian approach, we reach a midpoint in our lives when the identity that has been meaningful to us in the first part of our lives has reached a natural time for change.

In my case, I saw my identity as a migrant and an entrepreneur. This consumed a decade of my life. In my thirties, I spent my waking hours on pursuits and activities related to this identity. Even though my efforts resulted in favorable conclusions and I achieved the outcomes I hoped for, I found myself at a loss. I left the decade feeling unresolved; incomplete. Now what?

Talking to old friends at the reunion, I realized that I had become the least adventurous among them. Morris was going to Brussels the next day for Christmas, Miguel to Hong Kong. Stanley was leaving for a conference in Orlando, Florida. Louie was going to China for his son's chess tournament. I still find myself hesitant to venture outside of my box, to travel to other countries, for reasons like not knowing the language. I'm not confident about doing new things or traveling to unfamiliar places on my own, unlike before. What is next? What else is left?

The U-Curve of Happiness Theory

Economist David Blanchflower, with his collaborator Andrew Oswald, popularized a theory based on large-scale datasets on well-being and age across more than one hundred countries. Blanchflower's consistent findings across diverse populations highlighted the U-shaped pattern as a key concept in understanding happiness over the course of life.

The U-curve of happiness suggests that life satisfaction is high in childhood and adolescence, before gradually declining to a low point in midlife, around the forties. However, it gradually goes back up and peaks again in the fifties and sixties. This is because at this stage, people have gone through difficult times and learned to appreciate their lot in life, enjoying the future that remains.

Happiness in the Stages of Life

Youth (twenties to thirties): High hopes and happiness are often linked to family security and optimism, but identity formation and complex experiences can cause stress.

Middle Age (forties to fifties): The "trough" where happiness bottoms out due to maximum life demands or “role overload”, caregiving, career pressures, comparisons with peers, financial stresses, and unfulfillment of life’s dreams.

Later Life (sixties+): Happiness increases again due to gaining perspective, experiencing freedom from work, and finding contentment. This is marked by reduced stress, increased emotional regulation, and greater appreciation of meaningful experiences rather than achievement.

The theory notes that midlife transition is not a single crisis, but a multi-year period of reassessment and stress. The trend is also shifting. Blanchflower's newer research indicates that happiness levels for young adults (eighteen to twenty-five) are lower than in the past, potentially flattening or altering the classic U-shape for current generations. This is attributed to social media or changing life paths. Cultural variation also shows that the curve is not universal. Some rural or less-developed populations display different patterns, with recent studies suggesting the curve is now less consistent. (National Bureau of Economic Research)

I hoped for my sake that this theory was still true.

Our Lowest Point

> *"When we reach our lowest point, we are open to the greatest change." – Avatar: The Last Airbender*

Setbacks can hold value, however. Great things often come from difficult times. Carl Jung's midlife crises were shattering. His professional break with Sigmund Freud over a theoretical disagreement risked his career. He gave up his job as a professor and isolated himself.

Around the age of thirty-eight, Jung experienced profound psychological upheaval, which he called a "creative illness" or "midlife breakdown". This was marked by intense visions, disturbing dreams, and feelings of panic that led him to deliberately explore his unconscious. It was at this time that he birthed concepts like the collective unconscious and archetypes, documented in *The Red Book.* (Schultz and Schultz, Theories of Personality)

Jung's Meaning of Life

According to Jung, "The privilege of a lifetime is to become who you truly are."

The process of becoming one's true Self is life's ultimate goal: To discover one's unique purpose and fulfill one's destiny. To embrace individuality unapologetically despite societal pressures or expectations. The journey to authenticity is challenging but deeply rewarding, making it a privilege worth pursuing.

This involves knowing all aspects of ourselves, including the Shadow or unconscious — our hopes, dreams, fears, and wounds. Only then can we forge our own path by combining everything we have learned so far. When we look inside ourselves, our vision becomes clear and we no longer seek to just fit in.

Individuation

Self-discovery is a lifelong process. The goal of human development is to have a more complete and unified sense of self, to achieve psychological wholeness and fulfillment. The core concept of Jungian psychology, individuation, is the process of becoming a whole and fully integrated person by integrating the conscious and unconscious elements of the psyche.

It is knowing oneself as completely as possible and harmonizing all the parts that might otherwise remain repressed or underdeveloped. Thus, when a person says they are "out of sorts" or "falling apart", it indicates that the Self is not doing its job properly.

23, 24, 25

The reunion was on the twenty-third of December, a Tuesday. We each said our goodbyes and exited the restaurant one by one. The name of the restaurant translated to "Good Luck".

Wednesday was the day before Christmas. I had a nice family lunch with my mom and dad, cousins Edna and Imma, and Matt. I flew back on Christmas Eve. As such, I had an entire row to myself. Cocooned in four blankets and four pillows, I slept soundly and horizontally on all four seats. I was relieved to avoid the post-holiday rush.

Thursday was Christmas Day. I was invited to a friendly holiday dinner at Bob and Kris's. On the kitchen island was delicious turkey, stuffing, sweet potato casserole, and an assortment of desserts. Karen prepared an afterparty game to guess the names of mysterious spices, by sight or smell. I got zero out of ten. All in all, it was a busy and joyful season.

There is still life left to live after all, and an important process still to undergo — starting with learning how to identify and differentiate spices.

"The years teach much, which the days never knew." – Ralph Waldo Emerson, American philosopher, father of transcendentalism

Chapter 14

The Unlocked Door

On Suffering

We become different people over the course of our lives. Some people proudly proclaim, "I'm the same person I have always been." But this is often a statement made in youth. During your life, you will encounter seminal events and people that fundamentally, irrevocably, and unequivocally change you, down to your DNA. There was the You before and the You after.

You only have a modicum of control over your daily life, your job, your relationships with people. You are subject to the whims of others. The only thing that you can control is yourself. Even then, there are no guarantees. At some point, you might lose control over your mental faculties or your physical abilities, and your sphere of influence and the space you control could shrink as a result.

I didn't think it would happen to me, but I fell into the classic trap people often find themselves in after a life change like quitting or losing their job. Now what?

In situations like these, people are confronted with life-affirming or life-altering questions: What are the things you need that are important to you? Where do you want to be in life? When should you enact your plans? Who are you outside of the confines that shape your identity — whether it is a job, a profession, a relationship, a community, a geography, or an immigration status? How do you make life better? Questions swirled in my mind like a tidal pool.

Suffering

Humans experience suffering for different reasons. Throughout history, philosophers have sought to understand the nature of human suffering — the state of undergoing pain, distress, or hardship. They shared their wisdom with the world, and I sought out what they had to say.

Stoicism (A Question of Challenges or Opportunities)

Suffering is an unavoidable part of life. *Amor Fati* means to love fate — to accept all of life's experiences including the bad, painful, and scary ones.

According to the Stoics, the key is not to try to eliminate suffering, but to cultivate resilience and virtue. Stoic suffering isn't about enduring pain passively. It's about actively transforming it into inner strength. Often, we suffer in our minds more than in actual reality. Focusing on the things that we can control helps us to take responsibility for our own happiness and well-being. Key principles involve: Recognizing that suffering stems from our judgments and not events themselves. Using adversity to build resilience and virtue. Turning challenges into opportunities for growth and personal development.

Stoicism teaches us to free ourselves from attachment to fully experience life. Human beings get attached to their partner, material belongings, career, lifestyle, hopes, dreams, expectations, past lives, and future outcomes. The moment we get too attached, we become more vulnerable to being hurt.

This is because we try to fill the void inside of us with another object or person. We start to have expectations. We seek happiness in external sources. However, clinging to them can only make us more miserable.

Attachment is suffering, because everything in life is impermanent. We won't own anything or have anyone in our lives for long. Even our own time is limited. Thus, we shouldn't spend it by living with the burden of attachment.

We can reduce our suffering by: Controlling our response to unavoidable hardship. Accepting what we cannot change. Letting go of our attachment to outcomes.

Zen Buddhism (A Question of Pain or Suffering)

Suffering does not result from pain itself but from our resistance to it. *Dukkha* means suffering that arises from change. Even pleasant things like happiness and success can cause suffering because they eventually end as well.

Suffering is inherent to existence, due to the impermanence of everything. When we resist suffering, we create more pain for ourselves. When we accept impermanence, we open ourselves to the possibility of finding release.

Zen masters teach that the path to liberation isn't by avoiding hurt and pain, but by directly meeting and accepting them. This is through present-moment awareness (like meditation and mindfulness) to see the true nature of suffering, and realizing that clinging to pleasant or unpleasant experiences only creates further suffering. True peace comes from detachment from ephemeral things, not from changing circumstances.

Buddhism teaches that a person must be independent to have a meaningful relationship with another human being. Being too attached to another person causes suffering, which prevents you from living freely and happily. Once you simply appreciate them, enjoy the time you spent together, thank them for being in your life, and don't expect anything from them, you can cultivate a connection that will fulfill you.

Pain is inevitable, but suffering is a choice. You are the one who can either continue it or end it. The Buddha used *The Parable of the Poisoned Arrow* to illustrate the difference between pain and suffering.

> *It's just as if a man were wounded with an arrow thickly smeared with poison. His friends and companions, kinsmen and relatives would provide him with a surgeon. And the man would say, "I won't have this arrow removed until I know whether the man who wounded me was a noble warrior, a priest, a merchant, or a worker."*
>
> *He would say, "I won't have this arrow removed until I know the given name and clan name of the man who wounded me. Until I know whether he was tall, medium, or short. Until I know whether he was dark, ruddy-brown, or golden-colored. Until I know his home village, town, or city. Until I know whether the bow with which I was wounded was a long-bow or a crossbow. Until I know whether the bowstring with which I was wounded was fiber, bamboo threads, sinew, hemp, or bark. Until I know whether the shaft with which I was wounded was wild or cultivated. Until I know whether the feathers of the shaft with which I was wounded were those of a vulture, a stork, a hawk, a peacock, or another bird. Until I know whether the shaft with which I was wounded was bound with the sinew of an ox, a water buffalo, a langur, or a monkey."*
>
> *He would say, "I won't have this arrow removed until I know whether the shaft with which I was wounded was that of a*

common arrow, a curved arrow, a barbed, a calf-toothed, or an oleander arrow." The man would die, and those things would still remain unknown to him.

What happens after pain depends on whether we are in harmony with ourselves. Pain can enter our lives, but only we bring suffering to ourselves. We do this by overthinking, blaming, getting angry, seeking revenge, complaining, grieving, and reliving the pain. While life goes hand in hand with death, illness, and pain, there is no need to add suffering too.

Jungian Psychology (A Question of Meaningless or Meaningful Suffering)

Suffering is not necessarily a negative thing. Neurosis describes a tendency to cope with pain in an indirect or unhealthy way, rather than confronting it directly.

Avoiding pain leads to suffering. This is because pain is a signal that something in the unconscious or the "Shadow" needs attention. Suffering can be a vital catalyst for the individuation of the "Self" — the process of psychological growth, self-discovery and transformation.

Carl Jung makes a distinction between meaningless and meaningful suffering: Meaningless suffering (neurosis) comes from denial and resistance to reality. Meaningful suffering arises from confronting one's own inner darkness to reveal deeper truths about oneself. Meaningful suffering is necessary, while meaningless suffering is not.

The most significant barriers to a fulfilling life are often internal. According to Jung, we build our own prisons. Human beings can become trapped by their own minds. The walls of this self-built prison are constructed from unconscious patterns, limiting beliefs, repetitive negative thoughts, unquestioned fears, and self-sabotaging stories.

The way out of this mental jail and the path to freedom involves introspection, by consciously choosing new beliefs and actions, even if it feels uncomfortable and requires courage.

Letting Go

Satisfaction is never attained because there's always something "more" to desire. You hurt yourself by not forgiving yourself for things from the past, not giving yourself credit, not celebrating your successes, not following your dreams.

Dwelling on the past for too long leads to depression, while focusing mostly on the future causes anxiety. What we have is this present moment, and we miss out on life by not being mindful of it. Letting go of the past and future brings peace and freedom.

But the process of letting go is not a simple, straightforward action with a single, clear threshold — like walking through a doorway where everything on the other side is instantly different. It is not a one-time occurrence, and you can't seal the door behind you like in *Eternal Sunshine of The Spotless Mind.* There is no lock. The objects of your suffering always remain there in the back of your mind.

Letting go is a continuous act. It is an ongoing, conscious process of releasing attachments, grudges, and the need for control. It is a nonlinear progression of acceptance, adjustment, and healing. It means repeatedly choosing to stop carrying emotional burdens, rather than clinging to the past or trying to force future outcomes. It is our choice to walk through the door. In the same way, it is our choice still if we decide to walk back through it, for good or for ill.

The act of letting go requires kindness and patience with yourself, acknowledging that it is a long and winding path littered with setbacks, not a straight shot through an unlocked door.

"It is not the mountain we conquer, but ourselves."
– Sir Edmund Hillary, New Zealand mountaineer and explorer

Chapter 15

Granted

Resourcefulness in Adversity

"Granted" is a loaded word for some. Used in expressions like "Your wish is granted," "Granted, that is correct," "Granted, you are right," or "To take things for granted," it might be my favorite word in the world.

In Business

In business, a grant is a sum of money provided by an individual or an organization (like a public body, a charitable foundation, a grant-making institution, or a company with a corporate social responsibility mission) to an individual or entity for a specific purpose tied to the public good. It is a way for government to fund ideas and projects that provide a public service and stimulate the economy.

Of course, there must be a demarcation between government and commerce. Yet there are times when government conditions are especially favorable to business. During such periods, small business confidence and activity are high, as are consumer spending and grant giving.

Finding Opportunities

While in business, I was on the lookout for opportunities. I kept one ear to the ground, sought out business grants, and applied for them. There were public and private grants for different kinds of businesses, organizations and industries. I felt fortunate to operate a business in Washington State, which I believed to have a conducive and hospitable environment for small businesses. (Though others might disagree.)

Applications were typically submitted online, with eligibility, documentation, and essay requirements clearly outlined before the application portals were even opened. Required documents included items such as tax returns, specific tax identification numbers, income statements, proof of operations and sales, and answers to various essay questions or topics. Background checks were carried out to validate the accuracy of the information provided and to verify applicants' eligibility. I believe that being prepared, completing all the requirements, telling a complete story through writing in a persuasive manner, and finishing the applications expediently were favorable factors in the decision-making process.

Through Washington State Commerce, I was awarded a Working Washington Grant and a Washington Hospitality Grant in two separate years. I consider these capstones, as they were the first and last grants I received for my small businesses. I was grateful for these opportunities and didn't take them for granted.

Through the U.S. Small Business Administration (SBA), I was awarded a grant from the Restaurant Revitalization Fund, funded by the US Treasury. The program was introduced by the federal government to support the survival and growth of small businesses during a difficult period. Because it was a federal grant, it was exempt from federal tax, which was effectively like receiving a whole new grant during tax season.

Other programs such as the Employee Retention Credit (ERC) aided small businesses by affording them substantial credit for eighteen months. However, this program was not widely known. I received these funds, distributed by the Internal Revenue Service (IRS), by being proactive and taking initiative. I approached my payroll company and my CPA to start the process and worked with them to compile and provide the required documentation to the IRS. Half of the funding was retroactive, so some of the funds were issued as credits deposited into the business bank account, while the remainder arrived by mail as checks.

All these grants acted as non-dilutive funding, which helped preserve precious resources, with the proceeds helping fund capital expenditure projects and further investments in small business. In my eyes, these opportunities didn't come around often, so it was important to do my best to secure them.

On Resourcefulness

When I was younger, my dad fetched me from school on weekday afternoons. As the drive home was long, we would sometimes stop at the halfway point to go eat at a restaurant. Most of these places we went to are no longer there. One day, at a fast casual rotisserie called Henny Penny, he imparted his greatest lesson to me. He said that he attributed all his greatest successes as an entrepreneur to resourcefulness, and that, if I cultivated that quality, it could carry me through life.

Resourcefulness can, in fact, be our greatest resource. Carl Jung's concept of resourcefulness involves tapping into our inner reserves, seeing challenges as opportunities rather than obstacles, and trusting that meaningful resources emerge from conscientious effort.

<u>Embrace the unconscious</u>: Pay attention to dreams and inner

experiences to access creative solutions and deeper wisdom about life's dilemmas.

Shift from "having" to "being": True power isn't having resources, but being resourceful. Think in terms of possibilities, not limitations. Shift your focus from "having resources" to "being resourceful" through self-investment. Prioritize mental acuity, physical health, emotional balance, and intellectual growth. They are fundamental in effectively navigating life.

Do the work: When you truly engage in meaningful work, allies and resources (people, funds, support) will be drawn to you, rather than you chasing them. Stop wasting energy on draining interactions. Be mindful and direct energy toward meaningful goals instead.

Through Adversity

Hope pierces through adversity. Those days when I unexpectedly opened emails that informed me I had successfully secured a business grant were some of my best. It felt very surreal to receive some good news; some pleasant surprises. I could remember the rush of elation that I felt in those moments. I wish I could hold on to that feeling. It felt like validation for the many years of toil and grind, both as an employee and an employer.

Lotus flowers bloom in the mud. They push their way through the muck and rise toward the sun's light, a symbol of how something pure can emerge from murkiness and suffering. They represent the ability to rise above challenges, and the potential for profound growth to arise from powerful adversity.

Life's journey is sprinkled with positive developments and pleasant outcomes. There were times when I had to pinch myself and throw salt over my shoulder, because I just couldn't believe my good fortune. Good moments are few and far in between in life, but maybe these make up for the challenging and difficult times.

Rarely are there genies to grant our heart's desire. And if there are, we must first be able to draw out their lamps. I recount these tales as a reflection on how resourcefulness can be greatly rewarded, and how opportunity arises from adversity.

Resourcefulness is two million bagels baked over nine years.

Opportunity starts at midnight, while the store is closed and when the baker's shift begins.

Adversity is like the process of baking and preparing a piece of cake; it is only understood by those who go through it.

Part 4

Business

Chapter 16

Sugar and Salt (Part 1)

A Story of Opportunity

Tao of Water

In Taoist philosophy, water is the ultimate metaphor for Tao (The Way) and ideal human behavior because it represents flexibility, humility, and effortless action. Tao teaches that one should be like water: adaptable, nurturing, and yielding, yet capable of overcoming obstacles through patience and persistence rather than force.

The Way of Water means flowing with life and business circumstances, rather than resisting them.

Adaptability and Flexibility: Water conforms to the shape of its container, finding its way around barriers, rather than fighting them.

Nurturing and Humility: Water flows to the lowest, most humble places, benefiting all things without contention.

Yielding and Softness: Water can wear away hard rock, proving that gentleness through patience, persistence, and non-contention defeats rigid strength.

Emptiness and Openness: To be like water is to keep the mind calm and free from preconceived notions and self-imposed limitations.

Catch and Release

In business, Tao teaches moving with the currents, rather than swimming against them.

Much of business is about knowing when to hold on and flow with change, while also knowing when to let go. Instead of resisting, Tao advises accepting and moving along with challenges, as water flows around rocks. Instead of holding on to the need for control and rigidity, Tao suggests acting in the present moment, as bamboo bends with the wind.

The Business Listing

One unassuming day, I was browsing through business listings when I came across an opportunity to buy a company that produced, marketed, and sold confectionary ingredients for decorating, dusting, sanding, and glazing, along with flavored rim salts and colored glitters for cocktails.

The asking price in the ad for the small business was $ 149,000. Later, the Seller explained to me how they came up with this number. They took the annual net income of their most profitable year within the last three fiscal years, multiplied it by two, then added the book value of furniture, fixtures & equipment (FFE), and raw, in-progress & finished goods inventory. Typically, in such a deal, standing inventory is treated separately from the purchase price of the business. As such, the "actual purchase price" of the business without inventory cost would be less. I imagined that consumer psychology dictated the price of 149 rather than 150. Prices ending in nine are often more attractive to prospective buyers and may result in more inquiries.

I filled in my details on the ad's contact form and submitted it. The Seller, who turned out to be the owner of the business, got back to me with a non-disclosure agreement, which I expediently signed. He then promptly sent a brand and general overview of the company, containing more information about the business for sale, and we scheduled an initial phone call.

When the time came to call him, I was surprised that he had a call blocker that blocked the call. I assumed he was inundated by junk calls, since he was not selling through a business broker. We eventually connected after the small mishap. On the phone call, we discussed the history, profile, and future of the business. He briefed me on his background and goals for the company. I wanted to be mindful of his time, so I kept our conversation to a respectful hour.

Asking Price

Setting the asking price is a critical decision for a seller (and/or their broker). Positioning it at the higher end of the spectrum can help deter unqualified or nuisance buyers. Serious buyers can either agree to the asking price or negotiate a discount. Then, the Seller can make a counteroffer or simply accept the lower offer (since they have priced in a buffer with the higher asking price). The benefit of this strategy is the Buyer leaves the negotiating table feeling optimistic and enthusiastic. They'll believe that they struck a bargain. Whether that is true or not is a different story. Most professional brokers price businesses in this way.

Inversely, the Seller can push the asking price toward the lower end of the spectrum. The goal of this strategy is to receive multiple offers and cherry-pick the best one — with the possibility of inciting a bidding war among prospective buyers. In the end, the most competitive Buyer or the one with the greatest buying power closes the deal.

A Declining Sales Trend

The Seller provided me with a well-written and comprehensive brand overview of the business. It included the company history and a general description of their product lines, including qualitative information on what worked or didn't work in the past. It also contained a brief section on the company financials, which showed sliding sales year over year. This was key, as the sales trendline is a strong indicator of a company's viability and a predictor of future performance.

The Seller provided several explanations for the decline: the loss of a major customer account due to the natural expiration of a sales contract, as well as broad macroeconomic conditions, ranging from inflation to tariff fears, were also cited as reasons for the softened sales line. The Seller posited that baking sugars were not seen as an essential food staple, but rather a hobby for retail customers (like home bakers) and an optional marketing tool for wholesale customers (like restaurants). For companies, this included limited or seasonal promotions — and marketing is often slashed as an easy means to balance a company's budget.

The decline in sales was also attributed to a reduction in the number of stock-keeping units (SKUs) in favor of streamlining the product portfolio. This was observed to improve production efficiency, which in turn would reduce cost and stop-time loss. This assertion was proven correct in their profit and loss statement (P&L), which exhibited an improvement in gross profit margins.

The current year also yielded negative net income — another red flag. The Seller, however, reasoned that substantial costs were invested in research and development (R&D) and marketing. This was a deliberate effort to refresh the look of the product packaging and the Amazon store, including new marketing initiatives and promotions.

Valuation

The Seller asked what due diligence materials I would require from them. I didn't think it was prudent to give him a litany of requirements, as we had not reached that point in the business transaction yet. I just informed him of my one crucial requirement, which was proof of sales. This could include sales tax returns (which would be the most ideal), followed by bank statements, credit card merchant statements, or customer purchase orders.

In my view, the valuation of a small business can be based on either sales or net income (if the focus is present value). Sales are easier to verify through the aforementioned documents. On the other hand, net income is typically derived from a company's financial statements, which are usually unaudited. And those that are audited don't necessarily paint an accurate picture of the company's operational performance. This makes sales volume another valuable metric, as it's a strong indicator of whether a company is selling enough units to breakeven and generate positive income.

An acceptable purchase price for a business can be a percentage of annual revenue or a multiple of annual net income. For some, this is 30 to 50 percent of annual revenue or sales. For others, it's three to five times the annual net income. Ideally, both are taken into consideration, and the numbers derived from both methods will either reconcile or lead somewhere similar. At the very least, the average of the two can approximate a realistic return on investment (ROI). The ideal ROI for a small business is less than five years, if the intention is to carve out a livable income for the small business owner. Two or three years make an attractive rate of return. In the Boston Consulting Group's (BCG) *Growth-Share Matrix*, these businesses are called "cash cows".

There are exceptional cases where a business is valued based on its potential future value. These circumstances typically apply to companies with breakthrough innovations or patented technologies — industry disruptors that are expected to experience rapid growth and exponential sales. In the BCG Matrix, these companies are known as "stars".

The Reasons I Liked the Business

This was a new business model for me, which was exciting to explore. Whereas my background was in retail and food service, this business belonged in the e-commerce space. The majority of the company's sales were through Amazon. In addition, they also offered online ordering through their company website, as well as third-party retailers (Webstaurantstore) and wholesalers (Faire, GFS, UNFI).

I liked the fact that the products were shelf-stable with a long expiration date. (I had experience working with gelato, which is a very temperamental product that needs to be kept within a very narrow temperature range. Prolonged exposure to air also results in the sugar forming a sticky outer layer.)

I further liked that production was in-house. Unlike most online sellers or resellers, the company didn't rely on copackers. This meant that they had more control over cost, quality, and inventory. The raw materials (sugar and salt) were easy to procure. They had relatively stable costs that weren't prone to price fluctuations. There was an array of options for packaging material suppliers. Materials could be ordered from China, which was more economical but required longer lead times due to international shipping. They could also be ordered domestically, which was more expensive but faster to receive.

The business had a variety of product types in assorted colors, flavors, packaging options, and sizes, resulting in hundreds of SKUs. The products were sold in bottles and tins for retail stores, like gift shops, that displayed them on their shelves. As such, the presentation had to be eye-catching and attention-grabbing. They were also sold in packets for direct-to-consumer (D2C) channels, where value took precedence over presentability.

I liked that the production process had other potential applications such as pancake mixes, or maybe even body sugars and salt scrubs. Product diversity afforded the company a better protected moat. Growth potential was a big part of the reason why this company attracted so much attention. As an e-commerce business, it was not location-specific. It could even be integrated into an existing manufacturer's operation.

The company had multiple revenue streams and customer segments. It marketed and sold products under its own brands, but it also had a private-label (or white-label) program that allowed customers to apply their own branding to the products and even customize the packaging. They could then market and sell them to end consumers as their own products. In this way, the company acted as both its own manufacturer and other companies' copacker, making it a versatile operation. The customer base seemed diverse and large enough that the loss of one or two key accounts would not result in the near or total collapse of the business.

I was interested to see what qualitative data would emerge from breaking down quantitative sales data into (1) customer categories — retail, wholesale, private label; (2) customer channels — Amazon, direct, Faire, GFS, UNFI, Webstaurantstore, Walmart, etc.; and (3) customer segments — small, medium, large. This is the goal of customer analytics or a sales dashboard: to gather insight that could inform and drive company strategy.

Future Expectations

The brand overview illustrated the company's national footprint, which stretched from coast to coast. The products were available, sold, or shipped anywhere in the continental United States of America. Yet an opportunity still existed to expand customer reach and increase market density.

Would this business change my life and make me rich beyond comprehension? The answer was no. My best hope was to make a decent living from it. I figured there would be a lot of work involved (and a lot of sugar and salt to sell).

For me, part of the purchase price would go to education — training with the owners, learning in a brand-new space, and developing a whole different skillset.

The Offer

In his initial email, the Seller outlined the process for the potential Buyer to follow. If the prospective Buyer was still interested in moving forward after the initial phone call, the Seller wanted to be presented with an Offer or a Letter of Intent. On our phone call, I asked him which of the two he preferred. In my experience, a Letter of Intent, while more formal, can sometimes work against the Buyer, while a simple number can work to the Buyer's advantage. In general, you don't want to disclose more information than what is necessary. Anything could be used against you (much like in a court of law).

I ascertained that the Seller preferred a Letter of Intent, which would contain the formal offer amount. While the price is the most important piece of information for the Seller, the Letter of Intent also includes some other general provisions pertaining to the purchase and sale of the business. I presented the Letter of Intent to him on the same day as our phone call, which I think demonstrated my sincerity and eagerness to strike a deal with him.

My offer was higher than the Seller's asking price in order to make it competitive. I calculated my number based on twice the 2023 unaudited annual net income, estimated inventory, and the market value of FFE (rather than its book value). I also considered the Seller's Discretionary Earnings (SDE) reported in the general overview. SDE is a measure of a small business's total cashflow. It adds back the owners' financial benefits (such as salary, personal expenses, meals, travel, insurance, vehicle lease, etc.) to the company's net income.

I left some room in my ceiling price, so I could still go higher if the Seller came back to the table to negotiate a higher amount. My ceiling (which is a number that should not be disclosed during a negotiation) was three times the 2023 unaudited annual net income. A ROI of three years is ideal. I thought that it still gave me a small buffer, in case the next year's annual net income ended up being less than that of 2023. (A ROI within five years is still perfectly acceptable.)

Experience had already taught me that some business owners unscrupulously fudge their numbers, so everything should be validated and taken with a grain of salt.

The Seller responded positively to the offer in my Letter of Intent, though he sent me an aside in his short email. He reiterated that the listing had received a very positive reception, garnering a high level of interest and a large number of offers.

Chapter 17

Sugar and Salt (Part 2)

A Story of Engagement

A Tour of the Facility

The Seller invited me to visit the company's production facility one day at 4 p.m., after the employees had left for the day. I met with the two owners, the Seller and his wife, who gave me a cursory tour of the facility's premises. There was a production area with large barrel mixers; a storage area (which took up most of the space) with tall shelves stacked with raw materials, packaging materials, and finished inventory; a packing area with long tables where orders were filled; and a shipping area where pallets were dropped off and boxes were picked up by shippers or third-party freight companies. The layout was spartan. A small office had been set up in one corner, where I sat down with the owners. The space itself was open, with some tables, chairs, and various pieces of electronic equipment.

They showed me the new and improved packaging — part of a larger effort to refresh the brand. It featured plastic packets with transparent windows and barcode stickers for product labels.

The packaging was versatile in that it could be customized for the company's different product types and sizes.

The Seller told me that the business could be relocated to a smaller space to save on rent. However, some of the rent savings would be offset by one-time moving costs. A cost-benefit analysis could be conducted to determine whether a move would result in net savings. My preference was to reassign or renew the current lease. It would be easier and more economical to move one person to the business than to transfer a whole operation.

Near the end of our meeting, the Seller's wife asked me why they should sell their business to me. The Seller and I were both caught off guard by the frankness of her question. I told her that I respected the history of the business. They had built the company from the ground up as its founders, together with their employees. I would work alongside them to facilitate a smooth transition and carry their work forward into the future. I saw my role as a steward of their company who would nurture its growth and continue its legacy.

She also asked me what my role in the business would be. I said that I saw myself filling the gaps wherever they needed to be filled. If all the employees stayed on after the sale, I would be happy to assume a smaller role within the company. If one or more employees decided to leave, I could take over their job and work full-time or hire replacements. Whatever actions I took would be aimed at minimizing business interruption and avoiding complete disruption. Unless it became necessary, the external stakeholders (customers and vendors) would not even know about the change in management and ownership.

Glitter in the Air

At the meeting, I noticed that the owners were both covered in glitter. When I pointed out this fact, they informed me that they had worked with cocktail glitter earlier in the day. As the setting sun's remaining light cascaded through the windows, luminescent glitter hung in the air. It floated and oscillated, like a flock of birds riding on the breeze. I initially found it humorous — like there had been a big party or a rave on the warehouse premises.

Later, however, I relayed my concern regarding product handling, health, and safety. Sugar is flammable, and sugar dust could be hazardous in large quantities with repeated exposure. The owners assured me that the sugar did not pose a health or safety risk, as there was no cutting, washing, heating, temperature or chemical change involved. The process simply entailed mixing the sugar with natural food colors. Additionally, glitter is different from sugar dust.

The owners added that the space was properly ventilated, while optional safety precautions could be administered, such as face masks for employees. The facility was compliant with all state and FDA rules and regulations. According to the Seller's wife, their biggest safety objective was monitoring pests and rodents (such as ants) that could sneak in during sugar deliveries.

I liked that the production seemed to be a relatively simple and straightforward process, which was ideal from a profitability perspective. In general, the simpler the process, the likelier a business is to be profitable. It stands to reason that the more you produce, the more you can sell. Income is driven by volume and scale. Businesses need to sell products to generate profit, and there must be enough revenue to offset below-the-line expenses like rent and utilities.

Product Pricing

I asked the owners how the business priced its products, as I wanted to determine whether low pricing was contributing to their year-to-date net loss. The business had hundreds of SKUs, so it would be a continuous challenge to ensure all of them met acceptable gross margin thresholds and that the operation remained profitable. The Seller said that they used a spreadsheet with cost inputs to calculate pricing. These included direct, product-attributable costs such as raw materials, packaging, direct labor, and variable overhead. It is critical to keep a watchful eye on pricing, as the cost of raw materials and packaging can change at any moment. All the while, you still need to make money from the work you do.

Another important consideration is the pricing of competitor goods and similar or substitute products available on the market. How does your pricing compare? Are you priced toward the higher end or the lower end of the market? And does the quality of your products warrant the cost?

The Seller assured me that they had put in considerable effort over the past year to negotiate vendor contracts with favorable terms to reduce cost of goods as a percentage of sales. It seemed to have worked, as this was reflected in their most recent P&L.

I tried to be mindful of the owners' time, so we concluded our first in-person meeting after an hour. I felt encouraged by the warm reception I received during our meeting and the way both owners engaged with me. They were both equally vital in the decision-making process.

Mutual Agreement

In my limited experience, purchasing an e-commerce business is highly competitive. They are usually in higher demand than traditional brick-and-mortar stores. Not only do you need to contend with individuals in the local vicinity, but also with institutional and private parties from anywhere in the country. More people prefer online businesses over customer-facing businesses. They aspire to have the kind of business where the primary objective is brand-building. With a healthy dose of imagination, this can open the door to endless possibilities and limitless potential.

After our meeting, the Seller and I exchanged emails. They had narrowed down their options to three buyers, of which I was one. He presented a number to me and informed me that if I agreed to it, we could move forward with the deal. I decided not to negotiate and proceeded to respond in the affirmative, enthusiastically agreeing to his price. We were now in lockstep.

The Seller then sent me the purchase agreement and a copy of the existing lease to review. He also set up a second meeting. This time, it was with the Production Manager, the employee who held the most critical role in the company. Introducing employees to a new owner is very serious and should not be taken lightly.

The meeting with the owners and the Production Manager went very well. I learned about their working dynamic and history. I also listened to the Production Manager discuss what mattered to him and what would encourage him to continue in his role within the company.

I learned that the Seller was also the company's Head of Sales, and his wife was its CEO and Lead Product Innovator. I imagined the interesting tales that had led to the creation and evolution of their product lines. Innovation can come from the most mundane moments. It can strike like lightning, surprisingly and unexpectedly.

They had been testing, working out the kinks, and seeing what worked or didn't work over many years. They kept the products that sold and dropped the ones that didn't. For a healthy premium, buying a preexisting business carries considerably less risk compared to starting a new venture from the ground up. This is one of the advantages provided the Buyer does their due diligence in purchasing a viable (and hopefully lucrative) business.

I asked the Seller for three days to review the purchase agreement, after which I would send him an email with my comments and questions. I did so by said date. It is imperative to do what you say, in business and in life, as it demonstrates accountability and reliability.

The Difference Between an Asset Sale and a Stock Sale

Prior to our second meeting, the Seller sent me an email to inform me that the business transaction would need to be changed from an asset sale to a stock sale. Typically, in the case of a business sale, the business is treated as an asset to be sold and transferred from the Seller's legal entity (corporation or LLC) to the Buyer's.

While preparing for the sale, they discovered that Amazon did not allow a company's Amazon store to change ownership. (The tax identification numbers could not be changed.) The existing Amazon store would need to be closed with a completely new store set up in its place. This would entail the loss of existing history, customer data, FSA and warehouse records — all of which were incredibly valuable. Company history establishes the credibility of the business and affects the salability of its brands. It is easier to sell a product with a track record of verified purchases and trusted customer reviews. This builds awareness and top-of-mind recognition, not to mention the famous Amazon algorithm. It is also far more convenient for a repeat customer to buy again once they have made the initial purchase. Amazon is *the* online retailer in the e-commerce space. Consequently, an Amazon store was material to this business's ability to sustain revenue.

To that end, the workaround solution was for the eventual Buyer to purchase the Seller's corporation or LLC outright. The Buyer would essentially take over the Seller's legal entity, including its name, date of incorporation, and tax identification (UBI and FEIN) numbers. This would circumvent the problem with the

Amazon store. In the eyes of Amazon, it would essentially be the same company but with a different shareholder(s). And in the case of the Secretary of State (SOS), the legal entity would just have a different "Governor".

This strategy could cause complications down the road, as it would incur additional risks in the form of possible future liabilities. The Buyer (who would become the new owner in this case) would have to assume any debt, liens, encumbrances, claims, or lawsuits, pending or unresolved, even from the time the Seller (or previous owner) owned the company.

There were a couple of provisions in the purchase agreement that related to the stock sale. The first was a mutual indemnification clause for a period of twelve months after the closing date. This provided both the Seller and Buyer with some level of assurance that neither would be held liable for the other party, should something come up. The protection went in both directions. Of course, the clause had an expiration date, which is sound and true for any well-drafted legal document. I sought to extend the mutual indemnification period for an additional six months, just for added coverage.

Since I am in control of my own actions, I was willing to assume such risk. Not so for others whose actions I do not.

An Unrelated Asset in the Corporation

The second provision pertained to an unrelated timeshare, which the Seller owned under the same legal entity as the business. (A timeshare is a form of shared ownership of a vacation property, where a person or legal entity purchases the right to use a unit through a points-based system or for a specific period each year.)

The purchase agreement included a clause requiring the Buyer to sign documents related to the sale or transfer of the timeshare

— either to the Seller personally or to another legal entity — if the business sale were to occur first.

My initial thought was that the burden of risk fell on the shoulders of the Seller. A timeshare is an asset, and they were trusting the Buyer to cooperate. However, my perspective shifted after having more time to think about it. Timeshares have a notorious reputation for being incredibly difficult to sell or liquidate. They are known to be a potential sinkhole for owners, involving lengthy contacts, maintenance fees, one-time or recurring charges, or any special assessments. Not to mention the headache of having to deal with pushy or possibly tricky timeshare representatives. I knew next to nothing about the details of the timeshare, or where it was located.

Since the deal was now structured as a stock sale, this timeshare could simply be offloaded on the Buyer, who would have no choice in the matter but to deal with it. A timeshare could turn out to be a liability, as much as it could be an asset. The costs could easily outweigh the benefits.

Because the deal was now a stock sale, I felt it was necessary as a gesture of goodwill to ask the Seller if they wanted to retain a small stake in their company, now or down the road. This would be mostly ceremonial or symbolic, as they had owned it for over two decades. It might have held sentimental value for them. I saw it as an opportunity to formally retain their expertise and knowledge — other legal implications notwithstanding, of course. We also discussed the idea of extending an offer for a stake in the company to the Production Manager, if it would convince him to stay onboard. There are always multiple options to structure a deal.

Chapter 18

Sugar and Salt (Part 3)

A Story of Detachment

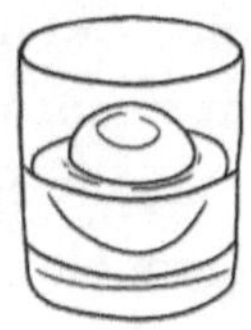

Earnest Money

The purchase agreement didn't require the Buyer to put earnest money into escrow, which was atypical in a business sale — especially considering the Seller drafted the document. At first, I thought this would benefit the Buyer, as they wouldn't be required to make a deposit or downpayment between the time of signing the purchase agreement and the closing documents.

After some time, however, I realized that the Seller would also benefit from this arrangement. They were free to continue shopping around for more beneficial or lucrative offers during the Buyer's due diligence (or feasibility) period. They could still advertise the listing and entertain prospective buyers, keeping their options open. At worst, the Seller could renege on the agreement at any time.

The Seller set a closing date just two weeks out. By that point, all contingencies would need to be removed, the lease reassigned, funds transferred, and the bill of sale executed. This also meant that the due diligence period would be quite short. I accepted this conditional timeline because the relatively low purchase price compensated for the higher risk profile.

The Sound of Silence

I carefully reviewed the purchase agreement and let the Seller know that it looked good. I listed my comments and questions (typos, corrections, additions, clarifications), but nothing material. I asked that the corporation's operating agreement and a noncompete agreement (which the Seller previously verbally agreed to) be included in the appendix. I reached out to a reputable escrow attorney for assistance in checking and verifying liens held against the business. It was prudent to use a third party, since they aren't biased or motivated to report anything but the objective truth.

I didn't hear back from the Seller for twenty-four hours, so I sensed something was amiss. Alarm bells started ringing in my head. The Seller sent me an email on Saturday stating that "some things came up on their end" and that they "hoped to make a final decision on the Buyer by tomorrow night". Final decision on the Buyer?

I suspected that the Seller was still shopping around for a better offer. It was likely that he had used my offer as leverage in drumming up interest and driving up the price for the business. If so, the Seller technically would not have done anything wrong. Thus far, we only had a "gentleman's agreement." Documents had not been signed, so no covenants had been breached or violated. Verbal agreements seldom hold water. All is fair in business.

The Intent Behind What Is Said and Unsaid

I interpreted the Seller's message as *you need to up your offer.* I saw no other reason why they would backtrack and mention the part about "(hoping) to make a final decision on the Buyer" by the Sunday night. He could have very well sent a general message without alluding to the involvement of other parties.

I did find it curious that they aimed to make their decision by that Sunday. I didn't think the weekend would give them enough time to arrange further meetings with other prospective buyers. In my opinion, it was simply a delay tactic to hook me while they tried to catch a bigger fish. Because of this, I didn't really expect to hear from the Seller by Sunday.

Nevertheless, I promptly responded to his email. I thanked him for keeping me updated on their process and communicated my understanding. After all, they had to do what was best for their business, their employees, and their family. I told him that I looked forward to hearing back from them, and to let me know if they needed anything else from me. I also informed him that I would be in town that weekend if they wanted to meet. I received the cold shoulder, and my message was not even dignified with a response.

Negotiation 101: You don't negotiate with yourself. As such, I intentionally did not give the Seller a specific number (of how much I could increase my offer). I left the door open by sharing that I was willing to meet with them. I could go higher. My standing offer was slightly below what I had budgeted, but first they needed to give me the number they wanted me to match.

They had employed this tactic before when I agreed to their price (thrice actually — first the asking price on the listing, second the price on the Letter of Intent, and third the price when it was down to three Buyers), so I understood their hesitance to repeat the same strategy. It was a tactic with diminishing returns. This play would only work so many times.

Placing a higher offer on the table would continue to weaken my position. At that point, it would accelerate a cycle of driving up the price until only one offer remained. However, it was also a precarious strategy for the Seller, since they ran the risk of alienating everyone they were negotiating with.

The weekend came and went. Monday passed, and I still didn't hear from the Seller. This validated my suspicion that he was going to use the rest of the week to arrange other meetings in an attempt to get the highest bid possible. The silence spoke volumes. And it was crystal clear to me what was occurring behind closed doors.

The Decision to Withdraw

Like the glitter in the production facility that fateful afternoon, my thoughts hung heavy in the air. I thought carefully about my next steps as I weighed my options. I deliberately slept on it (several nights, in fact) before taking any action that would likely be irreversible.

I admit I have often taken the passive approach in life. I tend to let things fall where they may so I won't have to make the hard decisions myself. Thoughts swirled in my head like the sugar in those big barrel mixers. E-commerce might give me access to a larger market, but it would also come with greater challenges — more competition, as well as a wider range of substitutes and alternative options for customers. The owners had the business for many years but didn't really have the profitability to show for it. The purchase price was almost at the point where the deal didn't make financial sense anymore, as those funds could instead be deployed in lower-risk, income-generating activities.

Sticking with the deal and paying more for this business would be a decision driven by emotion. If it merely broke even and didn't make a return on investment (from the purchase price and the Buyer's sweat equity), then the business would simply be a vanity project. Taking everything into consideration, I made a conscious decision not to react (by making an emotional decision in the heat of the moment), but to respond (by thinking things through and coming to a rational decision).

I concluded that I didn't want to play their game. I sent the Seller a brief and concise email: The fact that I hadn't heard from them led me to believe that they were going in a different direction. As such, my message served as notice of the withdrawal of my formal offer. I thanked them for the opportunity to learn about their business and wished them the best.

Denouement

Sometime later, I received an email from the Seller. He apologized for not getting back to me sooner. Apparently, they had sold their house around the same time — which made me question the thirty-day training period stipulated in the purchase agreement; I suppose the once-off or ongoing consulting arrangement would be remote... but I digress.

He ended by saying that he would "let me know if things change." This phrase validated everything I suspected. I was their alternative or backup option (and apparently continued to be). They used my offer to barter a better deal with another Buyer.

A month later, the business listing was still active and showed as "Pending."

Bar Talk

The Seller had previously owned another business, a bar he sold four years earlier. My friend was familiar with the place and met the bar's current owner, who had bought it from the Seller. This came as a surprise to me. I didn't connect the two because the current owner had changed the bar's name. It was doing very well, better than when his predecessor was in charge, and it was well-regarded in the community for its decadent food and drink selection.

One night shortly after I withdrew my offer, my friend and I went to the bar. It was an upscale establishment with a comfortable atmosphere: somewhere a discerning patron might drop in for a craft lager with a shot of Pendleton Whiskey. The space was well-appointed and decidedly classic — enveloped in rich mahogany wood, rustic terracotta brick, and the faint yellow glow of wrought-iron pendant lights. Large windows framed the downtown scenery. Sitting there, I thought this was unmistakably the best that the Pacific Northwest had to offer. Coincidentally, our bartender for the night turned out to be the distinguished Bar Owner himself.

The Bar Owner's opinion of the Seller was telling. He said that the Seller used to be a Microsoft executive and commercial broker before he went into business. It made sense, seeing how confident and knowledgeable the Seller had seemed throughout our interactions. When I told the Bar Owner what had happened, he exclaimed that it "sounded like [Seller's name]." Apparently, the Seller delayed committing to a deal with him too, even when the Bar Owner's offer was 20 percent above the original asking price. Our experiences seemed to line up (the major difference being that his deal closed while mine did not).

The Bar Owner also recounted an incident when he randomly received a phone call from some bank or lender, who said it was regarding an outstanding lien placed on the bar. (A lien is a legal claim on a property belonging to another person until the payment of a debt is secured.) He relayed this information to the Seller. Apparently, the Seller's reaction to the news was along the line of, "no one was supposed to know that." Still, the Seller handled the lien within a couple of weeks, and everything was free and clear for the Bar Owner after that.

Lessons in Business and in Life

The art of detachment: Don't get attached to an opportunity if the facts no longer make sense. Don't fixate on an outcome if the compromises and concessions no longer feel right. Are you acting out of fear, greed, or a need for closure?

An abundance of caution and an ounce of luck: No business endeavor is perfect, but don't be afraid to take a risk if it is within reason. Open the door when opportunity knocks, but before letting it in, engage and ask questions as a form of due diligence.

Everyone has an angle: Assume that everyone will act in their own self-interest. Deals close and businesses work when those interests are aligned.

Trust your instincts: Listen to the intention of what is *not* being said as much as what *is* being said. Think about the person's motivation beneath surface-level words and actions. Keep your eye on the forest, and not the trees.

Sugar or salt: Never rush, or you could mistake one for the other. Both have their place, but they serve different purposes. Sugar and salt look the same, but they taste very different; it would be like eating fish with a pinch of sugar or drinking coffee with a spoonful of salt.

Chapter 19

The Demented Dentist of Mira Mesa

Resilience in Rejection

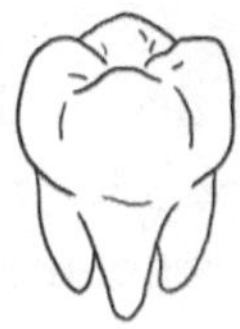

One blue morning, I received an email asking if I was available for an in-person job interview that same day. The role was an office manager at a dental clinic in Mira Mesa. The email came from someone named Kenny, who used Indeed for hiring. After pausing for a moment, I responded that I was available. In a matter of minutes, Kenny got back to me and asked how soon I could get there. The urgency to fill an office job seemed strange, but I decided to entertain it anyway. Most potential employers don't even respond at all. I let him know that I could be there at 1p.m.

A Dental Clinic of Mistaken Identity

I typed the name of the dental clinic into Google Maps and proceeded to drive to Mira Mesa. I got there early, so I decided to park and wait in my car. When it was almost time for the interview, I walked in and approached the receptionist. I told her I was there for a job interview with Kenny. She looked puzzled. The quizzical expression on her face told me that she was scanning her memory for the name Kenny. I wondered how many people worked there if she couldn't remember the name of one of her coworkers.

Suddenly, her face lit up. She informed me that I might be in the wrong place. Apparently, there was another dental clinic in Mira Mesa with the same name, except it was "[Name] **Family** Dental", whereas this one was just "[Name] Dental". She mentioned that other job applicants had made the same mistake in the past; it was a common mix-up.

I decided to call the other dental clinic to inform Kenny that I would be late and apologize for going to the wrong place. According to Google Maps, it was fifteen minutes away. A man answered the phone, and I explained my situation. He didn't even seem to listen to what I was saying. He plainly stated that any job application concerns should be handled through Indeed or email. I was taken aback by his curt disposition, but I didn't wish to argue, so I simply responded in the affirmative. Then he pointedly exclaimed, "Do you understand?" I could barely utter another word before he hung up the phone.

Bureaucracy in the Form of Job Application Forms

I decided to write Kenny a message through Indeed to inform him that I was going to be late and why. I drove to "[Name] **Family** Dental." This time, the receptionist instantly recognized the name Kenny. She handed me some elaborate forms to fill out. I hurriedly answered the questions and skipped those that didn't seem pertinent to evaluate my job qualifications. I also skipped the parts that replicated information already covered in my resume and cover letter, which Kenny had asked me to bring.

I returned the clipboard with the forms to the receptionist and went back to my seat. After a few minutes, she walked over and handed the same forms back to me. She highlighted all the questions I had left blank and told me that I needed to complete those as well. I was already late, so I decided to prioritize speed over detail. I hurriedly finished the forms so as not to hold up the hiring person any longer. I found it unusual that they asked details like applicants' social security numbers before extending an offer to them. What kind of business were they operating here? I scribbled my social security number illegibly, handed the forms back to the receptionist, and waited again.

The Surprise Exam

After a few minutes, she called my name and took me to a small room with three computers. She then told me that I was to take a test on one of the computers. I noticed an older woman taking a test on the computer at the far end of the room. How many office managers did this dental clinic need?

The receptionist didn't say what kind of test it was going to be. I soon discovered that it comprised three parts: psychology, math & verbal aptitude, and computer skills. Kenny had not told me about this, so I neither expected nor prepared for it. I did it anyway. It took about an hour, which was within their allotted time limit. I kept thinking that this was a lot for an office job at a dental clinic, but who was I to question their methods?

The Hiring Interrogation

After completing the test, I waited in the reception area again. Finally, a man who I assumed to be Kenny came to get me. (He didn't say his name at any point during our meeting — just like Rumpelstiltskin).

He directed me to his office, which was a smaller room than the testing room. Right away, I noticed his aggressive demeanor. Perhaps he was irritated because he had been kept waiting. Interviewing with him in that windowless office felt like an interrogation in a holding cell, as if I were a suspect of a felony.

He asked why I had checked "hospitality" as my industry. He seemed very agitated by that. I had scanned the industries listed on the form and felt like hospitality most closely resembled or described my background in foodservice, as there were no options for food, restaurant, retail, customer service, etc. Judging by his reaction, I later wondered if he thought *hospitality* had something to do with *hospitals*.

He asked why I had applied for this job when my previous experience was in bakeries. I answered that I'd felt encouraged to apply because the job listing explicitly stated that experience in the medical field was not necessary. That didn't seem to convince him at all.

He asked what I had been doing since the last job listed on my resume. (I noticed he was reading from my resume and not the forms.) I gave him the list of activities I had been doing, like working part-time as a baker, volunteering, and writing. He seemed combative once again. Maybe it was a cultural thing — like how some languages sound melodic and some sound angry.

He asked why the part-time baking job was not on my resume. I explained that I knew the owner personally and I had taken the job mainly to help Kayoko. He then asked why I was looking for a job, and why not just continue volunteering at Mama's Kitchen. I bit my tongue before I could say, because volunteering doesn't pay. I politely responded that it might be possible to do both, depending on the schedule, as volunteering was not restricted to business hours. I told him that I loved living in San Diego. I conveyed my excitement about the office manager's role; I was confident that I would excel at the job and thrive on the routine.

At the end of the interview, he asked, "Do you have any questions for me?" It had been a long day, so I just wanted to remain courteous and end the interview on a positive note. I smiled, apologized to him for being late, and thanked him for still seeing me and giving me an opportunity to interview. I didn't know if he had read my message on Indeed earlier because he didn't respond. He brushed off what I said and quickly snapped back, "That's not a question." That was when I realized that Kenny was the person I had talked to on the phone earlier.

As we stood up to shake hands, Kenny's demeanor suddenly shifted. He smiled for the first time and warmly bade me goodbye. I left dumbfounded. On the drive home, I wondered if his brash behavior was an intentional part of their hiring process — to observe how the applicant would deal with a difficult client. I asked myself if intent made it worse. And if so, would I want to work somewhere that used such psychological tactics on potential hires, or even employees? Was that acceptable?

Rejection

Rejection is a painful and powerful feeling. It means "change", and the brain doesn't like change because of the uncertainty it brings. When I applied for the job at the dental clinic, I expected to get it. When I didn't, a change took place: reality didn't live up to the expectation I had built in my mind, and that negative change produced mixed feelings. I returned to my car shellshocked. I didn't know what to make of the whole event. It was like a fever dream.

Mark Leary, a psychologist and faculty member at Duke University, explains that people who are rejected experience other emotions that are not due to the rejection itself, but to the implications of the event: Sadness when rejection produces a sense of loss. Anger when rejection produces a perception of injustice. Anxiety when rejection produces a state of confusion in distinguishing between real or perceived threats. Our emotional response to rejection is so acute because it dysregulates the nervous system. (National Library of Medicine)

Response to Rejection

Rejection is often an external event, outside of oneself. Stoic philosophy teaches us not to fixate on outcomes or dwell on things that are beyond our control. This alleviates the pain of imagined futures or expectations that we build in our minds but cannot influence.

Stoicism emphasizes living in the present, accepting the inevitable challenges of life, and appreciating what we have now. Recognizing that life will inevitably present difficulties and disappointments. Cultivating acceptance of these events, knowing that you have no control over them. "Time spent hurling oneself at these immovable objects is time not spent on the things we can change." (The Daily Stoic)

Resilience

Rejection is a painful and powerful feeling, but it can be used as a catalyst for growth through redirection and self-discovery. Rejection leads us to feel what it's like to be broken, to be lost, and to question the things that we believe. For many of us, it will happen time and time again. I have been beaten down by rejection too many times to count, repeatedly, before and after this event.

By facing defeat, struggling with hardship, enduring pain, and experiencing loss, we can master the delicate art of resilience — the gentle strength that comes from understanding that everything is temporary.

Chapter 20

That Store That Used to Be There

A Story about Decision-Making

A company in my neighborhood was once featured on the local news. I was surprised to see the "Store" featured — it was located in my city, so I recognized it right away. I had been there several times. I'll admit the news story fascinated me, and I found myself drawn in as it unfolded on my local affiliate.

The Store had been run by the same family for generations and had been beloved by the community for decades. It had loyal, multi-generational customers who came from far and wide to visit for holidays like Christmas, New Year, Easter, and Thanksgiving. Every year, festivities featuring a little reindeer "zoo" marked the start of the winter holiday season.

I bought holiday decorations for my own shop from the Store many years ago — trees, garlands, hanging décor, ornaments, nutcrackers, ceramic figurines, crochet animals, etc. I have kept them all these years and now put them up in my home every year. It's a nice reminder of a past life, and a continuation of an old annual tradition.

The Store was a local institution, woven into the very fabric of the community. It was part of the city's identity. When someone asked you where you lived, and you mentioned the name of the city, they would exclaim, "Oh, that's where the Store is!"

The Announcement

The Store made an announcement on the news that they would be closing in a few months. It was very sudden, leaving everyone surprised and shocked. I thought they would be there forever.

The company spokesperson explained the reason for the impending closure: the property owner they were renting from had allegedly reneged to develop the land. The Store had been intended as the centerpiece of an ambitious development project, which would have benefited the community and served as a key landmark for the city. The plan comprised of a mixed use residential-commercial area, a hotel and convention center, an entertainment center, and natural outdoor spaces. It would have been a major driver of commerce, jobs, and tourism.

A Brief History

I learned more as I delved deeper into the story. The Store used to own the property they were on — many acres of prime real estate. Its founder bought the land when he first immigrated and opened the business.

Apparently, they sold it at the worst possible time — during the 2008 real estate market collapse — for pennies on the dollar. It seemed they had made an unfortunate series of business decisions and, in doing so, lost control.

The Store made a deal with the new owner that allegedly allowed them to remain on the property rent-free for three lease terms.

With each term being five years, this amounted to a total of fifteen years of occupancy without any rent obligation.

And so, fifteen years passed, and the rental agreement reached its natural conclusion. According to the company spokesperson on the news, they started the process of negotiation with the property owner. However, they couldn't reach a mutually beneficial agreement that satisfied both parties.

The Buzz

The Store announced that they would close by the end of the year, after the holiday season. I suspected that they reached out to the media to garner public support, generate buzz, shore up the business for the upcoming holiday season, and possibly sway the negotiation in their favor. It worked for a while. People rallied around the Store, and customers mounted campaigns to raise awareness and save it. The media narrative pitted an independent family business against a faceless, nameless land developer.

The news also implied that they were being kicked out. However, when a reporter directly asked the Store's spokesperson for confirmation, the spokesperson didn't provide a straight answer on whether they were being unceremoniously kicked to the curb. They just proffered what seemed like prepared talking points. *We are in the process of negotiation and are hopeful for a resolution.*

My sinking suspicion was that the Store was asked to pay fair market rent, which would have a substantial impact on their profits and might have made their current business model untenable. Going to the media might have been the Store's strategy to try and get the deal they wanted.

Conclusion

The clock ticked. Months later, the parties returned to the negotiation table to see if a satisfactory deal could be struck. After multiple attempts, a deal still did not materialize. It seemed the property owner/land developer was not going to bow to public pressure and relent to the company's tactics. And so, the Store lasted a few months longer than they originally announced. It would still eventually close, however.

Liminal space now exists where the Store used to occupy — indicating a temporary change, a transitory state in the middle of two stages, a kind of purgatory between an ending and a beginning.

Three Universal Truths

In Zen, there are three universal truths: First, everything in life is impermanent and constantly changing. Second, because nothing is permanent, a life based on holding on to things or people will not make you happy. Third, there is no "eternal, unchanging soul" — just a collection of changing attributes and evolving characteristics.

Outcomes

It was an unfortunate situation all around. I kept thinking the Store shouldn't have sold the property in 2008. If only they had been able to hold on, they would have benefited tremendously from the explosive market growth and skyrocketing real estate valuations of recent years. On the other hand, there must be more to the story, and I don't know what their situation was back then. The most logical explanation is that they were overleveraged and had no other choice at the time.

I'm uncertain whether going to the news accomplished their goals, and I'm not privy to their inner workings. What I am certain of is that it was a complicated decision with multiple complex layers of consideration. From the outside, business decisions have to be made logically, weighing both immediate consequences, and long-term ramifications.

There was some buzz that the Store would relocate, but that never materialized either. Perhaps the family ultimately decided to move on.

In the following years, the big wineries in the city also closed. Like the Store, they were deeply embedded in the cultural identity of the city. I saw the city evolve before my eyes. But that is the nature of time. Something old must wither for something new to bear fruit. New businesses and entrepreneurs emerge from the ashes of old ones.

Part 5

The World

Chapter 21

'Tis the Season for Coverage Renewal

Tidings of Health, Tao of Insurance

Society

Human society is the collective system of people who share common governments, territories, and frameworks of rules and conventions. It is composed of complex structures that bring communities together, each shaped by common beliefs, customs, traditions, and values within a shared social or physical space. At its core, society is the web of organized institutions and relationships that enables individuals to live and work together.

I take interest in examining different social constructs, such as business, employment, the economy, finance, insurances, and taxes. Making sense of my own experiences within these systems is what led me to write these stories.

This Year

The holiday season coincided with the open enrollment period for health coverage in the coming year. I was all ready to renew my insurance plan with the same insurance company I had been using the last decade or so, so I merrily opened my Washington Health Plan Finder account online. What I witnessed on my computer screen knocked the wind out of my sails and sank my confidence like a stone.

My monthly premium was going to jump from $50 to $350 the following year. This was due to the expiration of the enhanced premium tax credits under the Affordable Care Act in December, which the government did not renew. No doubt millions of Americans were about to be affected by this.

I had just received a lump of coal for Christmas, but it could have been even worse. I qualified for the Cascade Savings Plan, which the state of Washington still offered, knocking $250 off my monthly premium. It was a gift, really. Otherwise, the same health insurance plan would have cost $600 per month. How did health insurance get to be so expensive? Wasn't that the point of it? To contribute an affordable amount in exchange for preventing financial ruin in the rare case of emergency or unexpected illness?

Several Years Ago

Several years earlier, right before New Year's, I flew to Miami for the start of the new semester after spending the holidays at home in Manila. December in Miami was magical. Twinkling speedboats cut through the water like comets streaking across the black night sky. That was what those days were like. The year flew by fast and fleeting. I couldn't hold on to those moments, but their memories lingered like mist that wash over a speedboat's passengers.

As a young adult, I admit that I was still ignorant about the concept of insurance. No one taught me about it. Like most people at that age, I thought I knew everything. But I didn't know how the country and its healthcare system, much less the world, worked. Thankfully, the university required students to have health coverage and facilitated obtaining it upon enrollment.

It was my first time living away from home. Growing up in a loving and supportive family was a blessing. And education was a gift. However, I was left woefully unprepared and blissfully ignorant of life's practical realities. I did not eat healthily at all that first year living on campus on my own. It was pizza and pasta from the fast-food restaurant almost every day, as it was the easiest and closest option near my dormitory.

Perhaps it was an unhealthy diet and not knowing how to take care of myself that led to my emergency that year. Or perhaps it was from the twenty hours of flying — sitting unmoving for that long can cause deep vein thrombosis (DVT) due to poor circulation, which can lead to potentially life-threatening blood clots. I had no clue.

I felt "off", so I decided to take a stroll outside. Maybe a little exercise would do the trick. Osceola wild turkeys and an alligator lazed on the banks of a nearby pond, while an iguana fell from a tree and plopped down right in the middle of my path. The guttural calls of blue-and-yellow macaws in mid-flight could be heard even from afar. It was still too early in the year to see snakes slithering all over the sidewalks.

I was on the pavement when I felt my chest tighten, and breathing became difficult. And so, I decided to walk to the urgent care clinic on campus. After running some preliminary tests, my condition was deemed serious enough to call for an ambulance and be rushed to the nearest hospital. This is the sequence of events that transpired.

Diagnosis and Treatment

(1) I had been experiencing chest pain for about a week when I would be still, and at rest. At the university clinic, I received an abnormal EKG reading, due to an acute inverted T-wave in lead 3 and a peak T-wave in V2-V3. This suggested that I was in a high-risk state for a major heart attack.

(2) I was then sent to Baptist Health for a blood test. There, my troponin level was found to be elevated, with a positive result of 7.11. Cardiac troponins (T and I) are the primary lab markers that enter the bloodstream when heart muscle is damaged and rise after a heart attack (acute myocardial infarction).

(3) The medical team decided to run a cardiac catheterization with coronary angiography, followed by a percutaneous coronary intervention (PCI). The coronary angiogram showed a small thrombus (or blood clot) in the distal part of the RCA, which was not flow-limiting. Its appearance was consistent with an embolic event rather than active plaque rupture.

(4) The following procedures were then performed to identify the source of embolism: transesophageal echocardiogram (TEE), color and spectral Doppler studies, moderate sedation, and telemetry monitoring. The TEE was the most terrifying of the whole ordeal, since I was still conscious when a tube had to be stuck down my throat. My medical records read, "The patient was given sedation with 1mg of intravenous Versed. The multiplane transesophageal probe was inserted and removed atraumatically. The procedure was well tolerated without complications." I begged to disagree.

The TEE revealed a 2mm patent foramen ovale (PFO). This is basically a small hole in the heart, which may allow blood to flow from the heart’s right atrium to the left atrium and vice versa, and may increase the risk of stroke and migraines. This opening persists throughout life in at least one out of four people.

(5) I was then taken to South Miami Hospital Heart Center for a coronary angioplasty to close the PFO. From my medical records: “The right groin was infiltrated with Xylocaine, and a 6F sheath was introduced with the Seldinger technique into the right common femoral artery. A JL4 catheter was then advanced over a J-wire, left main cannulated, and views were obtained. The catheter was exchanged for a right coronary catheter, right coronary artery cannulated, and views were obtained. The catheter was then exchanged for a pigtail catheter, introduced to the left ventricle, and ventriculogram obtained. The catheter was removed. A right iliofemoral angiogram was done.”

All this to say: After multiple attempts, it was concluded that the PFO was too small to close. The only course of action was monitoring and preventative care.

(6) For aftercare, I was referred to Gentiva Homecare, which instructed me to follow a high-fiber, low-cholesterol, purine-restricted diet. I had follow-up visits with several specialists over the course of the school year.

I was prescribed a boatload of medications during and after these events: aspirin (Ecotrin) for pain-relief, anti-inflammation, and anticoagulation, carvedilol (Coreg) for heart rate and cardiac function, fosinopril (Monopril) for blood pressure control, atorvastatin (Lipitor) or pravastatin for cholesterol management, cephalexin (an antibiotic), and anticoagulants/antiplatelet agents (or blood thinners) such as warfarin (Coumadin), fondaparinux (Arixtra), and clopidogrel (Plavix). I was also prescribed enoxaparin, which is a blood thinner administered by injection. It was a case of trial and error to determine which blend of medicines would work best for me.

(7) A torrent of letters, bills, and statements crashed down on me from different directions. My insurance company at the time, United Healthcare, asked me to obtain a letter from my last insurer, which was in the Philippines, certifying that I had no preexisting conditions. More than once, I needed to request a certificate of coverage to process my claims with my provider, which was primarily South Miami Hospital.

Beyond healthcare, I appreciated Americano, who lived with me in the student housing and helped me while I was incapacitated. I was also very thankful to my mom and Aunt Beth, who traveled long distances to check that I was well and taken care of. It meant the world to me.

Insurance

This was my first encounter with the healthcare system in the United States. It opened my eyes to the critical nature of social safety nets like health insurance, which is a lifeline in case of an emergency or unplanned event. I think like most Americans, I developed a healthy (or perhaps unhealthy) fear of going to the hospital, knowing how complicated and difficult things could get. The trauma and stress of the experience have stayed with me, also altering my diet and lifestyle since.

Bills from the urgent clinic, ambulance, hospital, laboratory tests, prescriptions, and doctors stacked up in an astronomical manner that left me breathless and made my heart palpitate. I was so, so thankful that I didn't have to pay the bulk of those bills (after my deductibles, of course).

It's ironic that a system intended to provide care and healing can unintentionally harm a person financially, mentally, and emotionally. How sad to think that the cost of going to the hospital can counteract its benefits.

How Does It Work?

In a word, insurance means protection. It is a contract where a person pays a regular amount or fee (called a premium) to an insurance company, which agrees to cover specific financial losses in case of an event such as an accident or illness. It is a way to mitigate risk and protect oneself from unexpected expenses — by pooling money with many others to cover a few losses.

By paying a small, *predictable* amount over time, you are protected from a potentially large, *unpredictable* financial disaster. The deductible is an amount you pay out-of-pocket before the insurance company starts to pay for a claim. However, insurance only covers what is specified in the contract (called the policy), so it's important to read it carefully.

Types of Health and Disability Insurance

- Health Insurance: Covers medical costs including doctor visits, hospital stays, and prescriptions.
- Disability Insurance: Provides income if you are unable to work due to a disability.
- Long-Term Care Insurance: Helps pay for long-term care services.
- Critical Illness Insurance: Pays a lump sum upon diagnosis of a specific critical illness.

Types of Property and Casualty Insurance

- Auto Insurance: Covers damages to your vehicle.
- Homeowners Insurance: Protects your home and its contents from damage or theft.
- Renters Insurance: Protects your personal property in a rented space.
- Umbrella Insurance: Provides extra liability coverage above and beyond what other policies offer.

The Arbitrary Nature of Rules

My annual physical exam has always been in January. I used to look forward to it every year to check that everything was as it should be. The year after COVID-19 started, my physical kept getting pushed back because of patient demand and, consequently, appointment shortages. Eventually I was seen in the last week of May.

The following year, the earliest I could schedule my annual physical exam was still the last week of May — exactly 365 days after I was last seen. My health insurance would not cover it if the time between check-ups was shorter than that. This is one example of the arbitrary nature of rules. Why should it matter, as long as I go once per year? (Especially considering health insurance coverage is renewed annually.)

Each year, the physical exam included ranking your depression on a scale of 1 to 10; an indication of the prevalence of depression in modern society. Based on your answer, the health provider can refer you to a therapist or prescribe an antidepressant if your symptoms have persisted for some time. I learned the hard way that you never know if or when depression and anxiety will hit you.

Years Later

Several years later, I had another, unrelated emergency that required surgery. At that time, I was enrolled in a cheap health insurance plan that, unsurprisingly, didn't cover my hospital bills. Luckily, Swedish Hospital offered financial aid, which took care of them.

Wu Wei

This is a core concept in Taoist philosophy, often translated as *non-doing*, *effortless action*, or *actionless action*. It is not about laziness or literally doing nothing, but rather spontaneity — acting naturally and intuitively, without overthinking or overdoing.

Wu wei means acting in alignment with the natural flow of the universe (Tao), rather than forcing outcomes through efforts that are ego-driven, forced, or unnecessary.

In nature, it is allowing a plant to grow at its own pace, rather than trying to force it through overwatering. In life, it is using minimal action to resolve a conflict or situation, rather than overreacting. In work, it is mastering a skill to the point where actions are automatic and effortless. (Campus London Limited, theschooloflife.com)

In healthcare, it is weighing options and considerations, like primary care physicians, specialists, providers, pharmacies, and insurance plans. It is making an important decision every renewal period, based on available data, and allowing the rest of the year to play out. Then, it is doing it all over again the following year.

The Final Decision

The expiration of the enhanced premium tax credits under the Affordable Care Act was out of my control, but making a thoughtful and deliberate choice was not. On balance, after considering the facts and my previous experiences, I decided that it was prudent to get health insurance. I found another insurer that offered an acceptable plan at $200 per month. It looked like it would cover my primary physician and medications.

To exhaust all my options and cover all my bases, I also consulted with a licensed health insurance broker through the official state health insurance marketplace. She came up with the same insurer, confirming my decision. At least I now knew that I wouldn't have any regrets about missing anything.

One never knows what will happen. Health insurance was a bitter (and expensive) pill to swallow, but it was necessary. It was my Christmas present to my future self.

The world is the people who reside inside of our lives.

Chapter 22

The Scary Letter

Minding Taxes, Taxing Minds

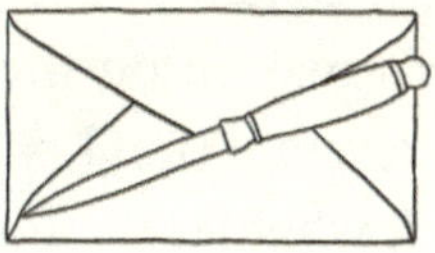

The Random Audit

Several years ago, I signed up for the US Postal Service's Informed Delivery Service. This service sends the recipient an email every morning with pictures of the envelopes that will be delivered to their mailbox later that day. That was how I found out that I had a letter coming from the Internal Revenue Service (IRS). I was lucky that I signed up for the Informed Delivery Service, since I had been staying in a different state for the last several months and would not have been aware of the letter otherwise. Thankfully, I could access the letter's content through my IRS online account.

I braced myself as I opened the letter. (Getting mail from the IRS is seldom a good thing.) The letter informed me that my business tax return from three years earlier was being audited. It claimed that I underreported my revenue in 2022, and so I owed upwards of $20,000 in back taxes and late penalty fees. The IRS reached this conclusion since the 1099-K form filed by the credit card processing merchant reported a higher amount than what I had declared on my business tax return. The difference in business revenue was over $50,000.

To understand how the IRS identified the discrepancy, it helps to know how 1099 forms work. A payer submits a 1099 information return to the IRS, reporting how much they paid to a recipient during the tax year. The payer also sends a copy to the payment recipient — one 1099 form per recipient. In this case, the credit card processor that accepted payments from my business customers was the payer, while I was the recipient of those payments.

The IRS takes the information on the 1099 form as evidence of the recipient's annual revenue (total or part of it). This is a way for the IRS to cross-check whether the revenues that a legal entity reports to them are accurate, which would affect their annual net income and, consequently, their tax obligation. There are different kinds of 1099 forms, including Form 1099- NEC, MISC, INT, DIV, K, R, and G.

The US Tax System

In the United States, the tax system involves federal, state, and local levels of government, including agencies such as the Department of Revenue, the Employment Security Department, Labor & Industry, and county governments. Each imposes a variety of taxes on income, sales, payroll, property, and other activities. The US tax system is composed of several key components.

<u>Tax Collection and Compliance</u>: The IRS is the federal agency responsible for collecting taxes and enforcing tax laws. The US uses a self-assessment system, where taxpayers are responsible for filing returns and paying taxes on time.

Progressive Income Tax: The US federal income tax is a progressive system, meaning the tax rate increases as a taxpayer's income increases. Income is divided into brackets, and only the income within a specific bracket is taxed at the corresponding marginal rate.

Types of Taxes: Most taxes can be categorized into three main types.
(1) Taxes on what you earn:

- Individual Income Taxes: Levied on salaries, wages, and investment income.
- Corporate Income Taxes: Levied on business income.
- Capital Gains Taxes: Imposed on profits from the sale of assets, like stocks or real estate, often taxed at different rates depending on how long the asset was held.
- Payroll Taxes: Imposed on both employers and employees, earmarked for social insurance programs like Social Security and Medicare.

(2) Taxes on what you buy:

- Sales Taxes: Levied by the federal government, most states, and some local governments on the retail price of some goods and services.
- Excise Taxes: Levied on specific goods such as fuel, alcohol, or tobacco. An example is Business and Occupation (B&O) tax for businesses in Washington state.

(3) Taxes on what you own:

- Property Taxes: Primarily imposed at the local or county level based on the fair market value of real estate and some business assets.
- Estate and Gift Taxes: Imposed on the transfer of property either as a lifetime donation or upon death.

The tax system in the United States is complicated and labyrinthine. I used to file my own tax returns as an employee working for a corporation and a small business. However, there was no conceivable way that I could prepare my own business tax returns myself. To illustrate, my last annual income tax return was more than thirty pages.

There were so many things to consider: evolving tax rules, complex and numerous "schedule" tax forms, depreciation and amortization methods, deductions (from tax credits, health insurance, my mortgage), the difference between short-term and long-term, actualized and non-actualized gains and losses, etc.

The Reason for the Discrepancy

Form 1099-K is an IRS information return specifically used to report payments received by an individual or a business through cards (such as Visa, Mastercard, or Discover) and third-party payment networks (such as PayPal, Venmo, or Zelle). One very important detail is that a Form 1099-K form issued by a credit card processor or merchant services provider reports the *total gross payments processed*. This amount includes not only sales revenue, but also any sales tax and/or employee tips collected from the business's customers. Sales tax payments are funds held by the business and then remitted to the State Department of Revenue on a regular basis, often monthly, as part of sales tax filings. Meanwhile, employee tips are part of payroll taxes filed, often quarterly, to L&I.

As a result, the gross amount reported by merchant services on Form 1099-K will always be higher than a retail business's actual revenue. This was not unique to the store I operated, so I was uncertain why the IRS would use it to claim that I had underreported revenue on my income tax return. (My audit took place around the same time the federal government and its agencies were facing budget cuts, so I suspected that the IRS agent might have been relatively new.)

The only time a Form 1099-K will perfectly match a business's actual revenue from card payments is if *no* sales tax or tips were collected. For example, a vendor that serves only wholesale customers (business-to-business, or B2B) typically sells to buyers who hold a resale certificate. This document exempts the buyer from paying sales tax on goods that they will use as raw materials or packaging for the products they make or sell. For example: Pizza restaurants don't have to pay sales tax on the pizza boxes they purchase.

Similarly, banks will issue Form 1099-INT to both the IRS and the taxpayer, reporting the interest income paid to the taxpayer. In this scenario, the amount reported on Form 1099-INT generally reflects pure taxable income, so it provides a clear and accurate basis for determining the taxpayer's tax liability.

Response to the Letter

I emailed my CPA to ask for her assistance in this matter, as I undoubtedly needed professional guidance. I felt like the accountant's professional fee would be well worth any potential liability or future risk with the IRS, which is not an agency to be trifled with. I prefaced my email to Brook (my CPA) with, "I just got a scary letter from the IRS." I trusted Brook and relied on her judgment, having known her for more than a decade through life and business changes, beginnings and endings.

The difference between the revenue I reported on my income tax return, and the amount of payments on the 1099-K was sales tax (which had been paid to the State Department of Revenue). To prove this, I needed to obtain all twelve monthly sales tax returns for that year.

Thankfully, I could still access my account on the State Department of Revenue's website. I downloaded the twelve months of sales tax returns submitted to the DOR and paid on time. Brook crafted the response document to the IRS, supported by the sales tax returns as evidence showing that the discrepancy in funds was in fact accounted for.

Thoughts about Tax Rules

Curious about other tax systems, and how they differed from the United States, I read up on tax systems in other countries. Whereas the tax agencies in some countries determine how much the tax filer owes, the US tax filer must calculate their own taxes and inform the IRS how much they owe. But then, the IRS will impose fines and late fees if they deem the tax return to be incorrect.

In a simpler world, the IRS could just tell you how much you owe in taxes, since it has the ability to determine this amount with documents like 1099 forms. Perhaps this is not possible due to the progressive income tax system or allowable deductibles outlined in the different tax schedules. I'm simply a tax novice, so I wouldn't know which method makes more sense. Each probably has its own advantages and disadvantages.

Tax rules are interesting because they're decided by committees, which can sometimes make them seem arbitrary. A great deal also depends on the state and county where the legal entity is based.

Take a bakery, for example. If an employee of the bakery heats up a pastry for a customer, they must charge and collect sales tax from the customer. If the employee hands utensils to the customer, they must charge and collect sales tax. However, if the store has a toaster for customers to use, and the customer heats up their own pastry, sales tax is not necessary. If it has a self-service station, and the customer retrieves their own utensils, sales tax is not mandatory.

Each individual business has the freedom to decide how to structure their operational guidelines, which directly impacts their sales tax responsibility. Some bakeries collect sales tax on all menu items across the board for simplicity. Some collect sales tax only on prepared menu items, not on "grab-and-go" menu items, which is allowable but adds a layer of complexity for the business. It does, however, save their customers from paying sales tax on the latter items.

Another example is purchase price allocation in a business acquisition. When you buy a business, the total price is allocated among tangible assets (such as furniture, fixtures & equipment, or FFE) and intangible assets (like goodwill). Most buyers prefer to allocate a higher portion of the purchase price to intangible assets to prevent business property tax. But some buyers prefer to allocate more to tangible assets because these can be depreciated, leading to tax deductions down the road. On the other hand, the allocation has no bearing on the seller. Purchase price allocation is often arbitrary because it is based on the agreement between the buyer and the seller, not the "actual value" of assets.

The income tax treatment of settlement proceeds is also not straightforward. For example, there have been class action lawsuits against credit card payment networks (Visa, Mastercard, Discover) over inflated interchange fees charged to merchants like my store. My claims were finally approved after a few years. Settlement proceeds have taxable and nontaxable components, depending on what it is intended to compensate. The IRS applies the "origin-of-claim" doctrine to determine taxability: A settlement payment which replaces income you would have earned is generally a taxable event. On the other hand, a settlement payment for physical injury, sickness, or property damage is generally a nontaxable event.

The Backdoor Roth

In the same year, I made my annual contribution to my Roth Individual Retirement Arrangement (IRA) account. There is a limit on how much you can contribute in a given year. The advantage of the Roth IRA is that tax is paid on the amount that you contributed for the year. As such, tax will not be owed on future gains or proceeds in your retirement account.

To make a Roth IRA contribution, the tax filer's annual income should not exceed the maximum threshold imposed by the IRS. The capital gains from my business sale exceeded the maximum threshold and thus made me ineligible that year. Brook notified me of this fact when she prepared my annual income tax return. I did not know about this condition prior to maxing out.

She presented one possible course of action: completing a Backdoor Roth IRA conversion, a workaround solution if your annual income exceeds the maximum threshold for that year. This seemed intimidating and complex when I first heard about it.

I called my brokerage company. The phone-support person helped me set up a Traditional IRA account. I then transferred the excess amount from the Roth IRA account to the Traditional IRA account. After the funds settled, I simply had to press a button to "convert" the same amount to the Roth IRA account. Doing so sidestepped the constraint. And that was all there was to it.

I Get Taxed, Therefore I am

In 1649, French philosopher and scientist, Rene Descartes, proposed a mechanism in which he describes how impulse leads to action. According to Descartes, actions from impulses operate through a specific neural path, called the "reflex arc", which includes sensory, interneuron, and motor components. This means that reflexes are commonly processed in the spinal cord rather than the brain. Because these bypass the brain for speed, they are considered as mechanical movements rather than conscious actions.

Reflex actions resulting from an external event or stimulus are thought to lack volition. Therefore, the actions of the body are automatic, involuntary, and unlearned, but the actions of the mind are deliberate, intentional, and meaningful. (Svetlana Masgutova Educational Institute)

Tax System Takeaways

- When you get the scary letter (an audit), don't avoid it. Take a deep breath, cooperate and work with the IRS in reaching a resolution or reasonable compromise.
- Be responsive: A reflex is automatic and something you are conditioned to do without conscious thought. A reaction is conscious and driven by emotion, such as fight (saying the first thing that pops into your mind), flight (leaving the room), freeze (saying nothing), or fawn (agreeing to avoid further conflict). A response is conscious and guided by emotional intelligence (answering calmly and deliberately with mental faculty after taking time to think about something).
- Respond on time: Different taxes follow different schedules. For example, property taxes on real estate may be due annually in April or semiannually in April and October. For most businesses, sales tax returns are filed monthly, payroll tax returns quarterly, and income tax returns annually in April.
- Consult a professional if necessary. It will be worth it in the end. If you decide to do your taxes yourself, be

cognizant of how the tax system operates and ensure that you work within it. Consistency and documentation are twin keys to successful tax preparation.

The mind can be a scary place to wander in for too long.

Chapter 23

Harbor from The Storms

A Process for Journaling and Writing

Writing is many things. It can be as small and weightless as dandelion fuzz. An idea floats and sways in the air, and you hope to catch it, before it completely disappears into the ether. Sometimes it lands on your nose. Sometimes it lies at your fingertips. Sometimes it drifts out of reach. It can be nothing or it can be something.

It is a puzzle. Nothing makes sense, so you decide to step away. But you come back to it, when something clicks. A breakthrough occurs. Random events and experiences start to make sense. Pieces snap into place, with each word carefully chosen and each punctuation mark properly positioned. The words form sentences, and the sentences become paragraphs. You continue to move them around until you step back, and the big picture comes into view. Then, you move on to the next puzzle.

Writing is a lone torch in a dark, pitch-black forest, pushing back the shadows and keeping tigers at bay. It is a playful orange kitten inside a safe space, drawing your time and attention and distracting you from your own worries and cares.

It is a loom on which you create something complex, like weaving a quilt from once-disparate patches. It is a sieve through which ideas and stories are continually refined, much like panning for gold from paydirt in a stream.

Writing is a floodgate; a means of shutting out, admitting, or releasing percolating thoughts and concerns — anxiety, depression, excitement, frustration. All your once-abstract, intangible emotions are given form and allowed to flow out safely. And in so doing, the dam does not break.

It can be as big and all-encompassing as the universe. It can encapsulate one person's lifetime, or the entirety of a society's existence. It is written history, a book of destiny. It can occupy the mind and become everything.

The Johari Window

The Johari window model is a tool used to improve self-awareness and personal development by enhancing communication between individuals in a group and facilitating the exchange of feedback. The name *Johari* comes from combining the first names of American psychologists Joseph Luft and Harry Ingham, who developed the model in 1955.

The Johari Window is represented as a window with four panes. Two panes represent what is known or unknown to oneself, while the other two represent what is known or unknown to others. The information is transferred from one pane to the other through mutual trust.

The four windowpanes are:

1. <u>Open area</u>: Information about the person that is known to them as well as others, including their behaviors, personalities, views, and skills. This is the main area where communication between oneself and others occurs.

2. Blind spot: Information that is known to others but unknown to oneself. Others may have a different interpretation of a person's thoughts, words, and actions. The blind spot is reduced through effective communication and feedback from others.
3. Hidden area: Information that is known to oneself but kept hidden from others. This is the private information a person feels reluctant to reveal, including their true emotions, feelings, fears, or secrets.
4. Unknown area: Information about the person that is unknown to them as well as others, including the qualities, capabilities, or talents they are unaware of. This can be due to past events or traumatic experiences, which can remain unknown for a lifetime.

Feedback solicitation is the process of understanding and listening to communication from others. In this way, an individual's open area can be increased, decreasing their blind spot and unknown area.

To me, writing and journaling serve different purposes in the Johari Window. Writing gives me the opportunity to communicate my feelings to others (open area), whereas through journaling, I communicate my feelings to myself (hidden area).

(Communication Theory, communicationtheory.org)

The Three Hearts

"There's a saying out here that every man has three hearts. One in his mouth, for the world to know. Another in his chest, just for his friends. And a secret heart buried deep where no one can find it. That is a heart a man must keep hidden if he wants to survive." – James Clavell's *Shōgun*

According to the Japanese proverb which inspired this quote, the first heart is the public persona, the face presented to strangers, often curated for approval. The second heart is the private identity, the personality shared with close friends and family, showing more vulnerability. The third heart is the most authentic self, kept hidden from all, for protection and survival.

As human beings, we play different roles for different audiences all through our lives. But our deepest self is guarded as an act of self-preservation. It is reserved only for us. Journaling allows compartmentalization, so we may safely explore that which is in our third heart — the hidden, unknowable heart.

The Philosophy of Journaling

In Stoicism, the act of journaling is more than simply keeping a diary. This everyday practice is itself an expression of the philosophy: Reading back on our daily experiences. Reflecting on the events of the day. Reminding ourselves of the wisdom we learned from our teachers and the people we met. Preparing for tomorrow's activities.

I draw inspiration from the ancient Stoics: Seneca (a playwright and political advisor from modern-day Córdoba, Spain, 4 BC–AD 65), Epictetus (a former slave turned teacher from Hierapolis in Phrygia, AD 50–135), and Marcus Aurelius (Roman emperor and philosopher, AD 121–180).

According to Stephen Hanselman, co-author of *The Daily Stoic*: "The Stoics weren't bereft of emotion. They just wanted to eliminate toxic emotions and replace them with good emotions, which included rational wishing (as opposed to blind hope) and rational caution (as opposed to blind fear). The bedrock of Stoic philosophy is an optimistic view of the human personality."

The Goal of Journaling

"The primary indication of a well-ordered mind is a man's ability to remain in one place and linger in his own company." – Seneca

Journaling brings about tranquility through reflective meditation. It also facilitates negative visualization, which is the practice of intentionally imagining potential negative outcomes like loss or failure. Doing this can reduce negative emotions: What is the worst thing that can happen? Would it be so bad if it did happen?

Through journaling, we improve our emotional regulation by gaining understanding of the source of our distress. Our self-control is improved by developing greater awareness in the face of adversity and practicing acceptance. In so doing, we cultivate mental clarity, emotional resilience, and a sense of purpose.

Franz Kafka, the Writer

"I wanted to escape the unrest, to shut out the voices around me and within me, so I write." – Franz Kafka

Franz Kafka (1883–1924) was an Austrian novelist and short-story writer. He trained as a lawyer and worked full-time at an insurance company. Despite only writing in his spare time, he is regarded as one of the most important literary figures of the twentieth century. His most widely known stories include *The Metamorphosis* and *The Trial.* Only a few of his works were published during his lifetime.

He once famously said, "Each of us has his own way of emerging from the underworld, mine is by writing. That's why the only way I can keep going, if at all, is by writing, not through rest and sleep. I am far more likely to achieve peace of mind through writing than the capacity to write through peace."

Kafka wrote about a person's need for self-expression, whether it be through writing or something else. To him, writing was an essential creative outlet because it was his way of processing the world and his emotions. When this outlet was blocked, it caused him significant internal conflict. He suggested that not pursuing a person's intrinsic passion and purpose can lead to psychological distress, a sense of incompleteness, or even "insanity".

When one is at peace with oneself, writing is what rouses happiness from within.

The Author, the Castaway

I am a marooned stranger, dropped in the middle of the roiling ocean's chaos. I cannot make sense of up and down, above and below. The clouds are dark, and the water is choppy.

Miraculously, I make it to land. Soaked and breathless, I gulp big swigs of air. A modest cabin sits along the shoreline, and I step through the creaking wooden door. Inside, a fireplace rests.

An idea sparks. It is so small that it fits in the palm of my hand. Husk, kindling, sticks on the flame. I blow on it, cradle it in the nook of my arm, sway it, continue to apply oxygen in the hope that it will catch fire.

It does, but the kindling does not sustain it. The little fire dies, and everything is cold and dark once more. I persist and try again. Do things a little different, adjust each time and refine the process. Flint, friction, fuel. Pen, paper, pages — all the same. The fire ignites again and grows slowly yet surely.

It blazes until the idea becomes an inferno. It is safe and warm inside the cabin. The smoke billows from the chimney as the wind carries my message to the eternal sky. The cabin is aglow from the roaring life of the fireplace. It is quiet and still in this moment. Inside, the fire crackles. Outside, the tempest rages.

"There is a pleasure in the pathless woods,
There is a rapture on the lonely shore,
There is society, where none intrudes,
By the deep sea, and music in its roar:
I love not man the less, but Nature more."
– Lord Byron, British poet

Chapter 24

The Little Dog That Could

Life's Faithful Guide

Bruce was the paragon of contentment. He was a small black Scottish terrier-mix with bushy eyebrows, a scruffy muzzle, and triangular ears that stood upright. His wiry coat was predominantly black, though it had begun to gray with age and whiten at the extremities. Thick tufts of hair sprouted from his ears, like those of an old man. And, like a dignified old man, he had a loyal, stoic nature — reserved with strangers but deeply dedicated to his person.

Cousins to Westies and Yorkies, Scotties are known for being strong-willed and independent. But they are also affectionate companions who love being close to their families. Like most Scotties, Bruce wasn't a cuddler, but he enjoyed being near his people and would happily sit beside them on the couch.

All dogs are different. Bosco was an easygoing, calm, and good-natured dapple dachshund. He would sit beside his person in cafés for hours without getting bored.

Willow was a husky-German shepherd mix. She was high-energy and high-maintenance. She was outgoing and liked to play with other dogs. But like a typical husky, she complained a lot. Her brother, Wiley, was human-oriented and liked walking to the dog park with his owner, always pleading to play fetch with his favorite ball.

Winston was a great big poodle, and Ruffles was a beautiful golden retriever. She was the best girl one could hope for.

The House

Separation anxiety is leaving for the day, to go to work or take a trip. Our pets' patience knows no bounds. They can remember and wait for us their whole lives.

Sadness is a pet's passing away. We hold their entire lives within a small fraction of ours. But sadder still is when their person leaves before them. I can't fathom the feeling they must endure, of being abandoned, forgotten, confused, scared, lost. They do not know whether the choice was ours to make. They are loved and cared for their whole lives, when suddenly, their whole world can be gone in an instant.

Time passes, seasons change. Dogs age, but so do their humans. Bruce's person passed, and so, the little Scottie would go live with her son. Inside their house, Bruce situated himself and made a nest of pillows and towels, like a child's fort. After it passed his safety inspection, he laid down his weary head and slept. In this space, he was safe and secure. Dogs are remarkable in their resilience.

Bruce now also lived with his "nephew", a caramel chihuahua that was as sweet as the candy, precious like a gold nugget, and vital as sunshine. Charles, with his luxurious, cashmere-like fur, liked to curl up to snuggle with humans. But he also had an independent and territorial streak, often resource guarding and protecting his things. He was smart and stubborn, eager to explore on his own and make new friends, unlike Bruce, who stayed behind, and stuck close to his person like a persistent sticker burr.

Outdoor Adventures

Bruce happily followed his person on his indoor and outdoor adventures, and he quickly adapted to his new active lifestyle. In his crate in the back of the car, his happy face would appear in the rearview mirror, tongue hanging out as he looked at his person in the driver's seat. He always insisted on standing, so whenever the car took a sharp turn, he would slip and slide from side to side.

Once, he was left at camp while his person went on a hike. The whole time he was away, Bruce frantically barked and ran around in circles, vehemently searching for his person. He ran as fast as his little legs could carry him. Nothing could deter him. When his person came back, Bruce acted like nothing happened, but he was so relieved. He still had a happy smile on his face, with his funny little personality.

Whenever they were out, the little dog didn't even have to be leashed. He would just trot along, following wherever his person went. Because Bruce had become hard of hearing, he needed his person in sight at all times. He was single-minded and singular in his devotion.

The Temporary Stay

Some time passed, and once again, Bruce's life shifted. His person went on a trip, so the little dog was left with a neighbor who had a little ranch. The neighbor was nice enough and even trimmed his fur. However, it was clear to all that Bruce was not happy. It was said that he was snippy with the neighbor's kids and didn't get along with their other animals. All he wanted was to go back to his person.

The Move

Eventually, one fateful day, Bruce was reunited with his person again, and he was happy. It didn't matter to him where they were or where they went, as long as they were together. And so, the time came to move again.

It had been raining for many days, and the roof started to leak in their new house. Bruce looked up at the leaking roof, then looked at his person, then looked up at the leaking roof again as if questioning it. His person laughed heartily.

In the dry summer, his person went up on the roof to fix the leak. Inside the house, Bruce supervised the renovation and repair. He was as excited as ever just to be included.

In their new home, Bruce dutifully inspected his territory in emerald fields of green, alive with all the exciting scents of nature and bright yellow wildflowers in the spring. He ran laps around the yard at full speed, raising both front legs first, then his hind legs.

The little dog was very food-motivated and loved his chicken treats. He appreciated his bath time and grooming sessions, even as he shook and shivered. Wrapped and dried in freshly laundered cotton towels, his happy expression seemed to exclaim, "Look how clean I am!"

Days and Nights

More time passed. Bruce was getting on in age. He developed summer allergies, skin irritations, and had little accidents. People thought he would be winding down, but he was the little dog that could. He seemed to lap water from the bowl of youth, enjoying what are supposed to be his retirement years and having the best time of his life.

The little dog was the happiest and most alive he had ever been. He didn't even know he was getting older. He just appreciated every moment for what it was. Through life's changes and chapters, ordinary and not-so-ordinary days, Bruce remained constant and consistent.

Inside the house, Bruce patiently waited for his person for their next grand adventure. In his restful slumber, he dreamt of endless bright days with his person that seemed to stretch forever.

The Black Dog

Dogs dream of humans, but humans also dream of dogs. In our human dreams, dogs often represent loyalty, protection, and vigilance. They can also function as psychopomps — symbols of faithful guides through the unconscious. Dogs can often appear as protective escorts, guiding the conscious mind during personal transitions, psychological transformations, and the process of individualization.

In Jungian psychology, dogs symbolize the instinctual Self. The appearance of a dog in a dream is often considered a positive omen. It can symbolize a harmony of instincts — an integrated, balanced relationship between the rational human mind (consciousness) and the raw, untamed animal instinct (the unconscious).

While often positive, they can also represent the "black dog" of depression or the devouring nature of the Shadow. In Goethe's *Faust*, the "black poodle" is a manifestation of Mephistopheles. Jung interpreted it as an embodiment of the Shadow that must be confronted and integrated. In mythology, figures like Anubis and Cerberus serve as guardians of the dead. Jung associated them with the psychological process of dying and, in turn, rebirth. (Joseph Lee, Lisa Marchiano, and Deborah Stewart, thisjungianlife.com)

Two dogs inside tafoni (honeycomb-like openings in rock), photographed by Doug Fordice.

Chapter 25

A Year in The Pacific Northwest

The Cascade of Time

Winter in Seattle

A boundless blue morning signaled the start of the weekend.

A clowder of cats, together with their humans, gathered at the Seattle Center Exhibition Hall for the annual cat convention. The much-awaited event was a celebration of the animal companions that bring humor, levity, and silliness to the monotony of human life. For thousands of years, humans have observed cats observing humans. They are quiet philosophers, pondering the questions of life and the mysteries of the universe — only with fur, whiskers and paws.

Capitalism hummed like a steady, low-pitched purr in the pet economy. Fans eagerly anticipated the official merchandise commemorating the occasion. Arrays of food, toys, and other cat essentials were everywhere, as well as cat-related art, apparel, accessories, souvenirs, and other not-so-essential knickknacks for humans. The jubilee was as much for humans as it was for pets. Games, costume competitions, and trivia contests were scheduled over the weekend to bring people together in their common interests. Several nonprofits were present to raise donations, spread awareness, and support important causes. Off in the distance, the Space Needle towered over Jet City. The month was November.

—

The afternoon hastened to darken as the daylight hours shrank with each passing day. The pace of life quickened. People carried rustling bags as they hurried between stops, checking items off their lists.

Outside, the Christmas Market was ready to receive its visitors. Sponsors merrily invited passersby into their booths to hand them gingerbread cookies and pretzels. Lufthansa held a raffle for a trip to Germany. Near the entrance was a wishing forest. Rows of evergreen trees stood stoic and tall, greeting the hopeful crowds. They scribbled their wishes on round pieces of craft wood and closed their eyes as they hung the ornaments on branches with string. Hundreds of white twinkling lights illuminated the pathways, like an evening stroll inside the blur of a midnight dream.

Yule was the season of giving, and people looked for things that sparked joy. Vendors neatly organized the wares inside their stalls. The clinking of mason jars filled with artisanal jams made from fruit ripened and harvested in summer sounded through the air. Matryoshka dolls, nutcrackers, and sparkling stars adorned the walls, their colorful, whimsical designs long inspiring art, music, and storytelling. Polish ceramic pottery, wax candles, and wooden ornaments were arranged on tables, while leather accessories and wool sweaters lined the shelves. Each unique item reflected the craftmanship and care behind its making.

Like a bustling colony of ants, lines of people formed as they awaited their turn to buy things to drink and eat. The steam from hot cider and *Kinderpunsch* rose into the cold night air. People clutched hot paper cups to warm their hands and sipped spiced beverages to warm their spirits. The scent of roasting Bavarian nuts wafted through the air, tickling the senses. Behind a glass window, a vendor was swirling warm pasta noodles into a giant wheel of aged Italian cheese. Another was busily making rich, melty raclette sandwiches. An assembly line prepared chimney cakes baked over an open flame. The golden spiral pastries were soft on the inside and crispy on the outside, and coated in sweet toppings like pistachio or Nutella.

Holiday music and breathless laughter emanated from the Christmas Pyramid that was shaped like a children's toy. Crowds gathered to listen to lively performances on the flying stage and sing along to nostalgic carols. Friends shouted "*Prost*!" to each other as they shared the magic of festive cheer. The month was December.

—

The walk felt long as night fell. A numbing cold spread through the body from the biting marine air. Red and green lights flickered, signaling the stop and go of pedestrians, as they walked in different directions across the city. A small boy held hands with Buoy, the blue sea troll with hair like the waves of the Puget Sound, said to be the nephew of the Fremont Troll, a Seattle landmark.

More people appeared as the Climate Pledge Arena drew nearer, many dressed in the same deep-sea blue, ice blue, and red alert. Others wore red, black, and white, the colors of the opposing team.

In the epicenter, thousands of people congregated with fanfare as pomp and circumstance preceded the game. Blue shards of light flashed across every surface of the venue as a giant sculpture resembling a Dale Chihuly piece descended on the rink. It was shaped like a giant tentacle of the mythical, mysterious Kraken, lurking beneath the surface and now breaking through the ice.

Symbolism is powerful. The folklore of giant Pacific octopuses evokes Seattle's maritime history and Scandinavian heritage. In that spirit, the team was named after the Nordic sea-monster to honor the region's deep waters and reflect the sea's aggressive nature.

Tradition binds people together to form tight-knit communities built on shared ideals and purpose. For a few hours, in a place where they felt a sense of belonging, people experienced the full sweep of human emotion: the pinnacle of achievement, the pride of besting others, the thrill of feeling alive, the call-and-response of elation in victory and agony in defeat.

The click-clack of sticks striking puck, the whistle of blades carving ice, and the push-and-pull chorus of cheers meeting taunts hummed in the air. The month was January.

—

The month was February. Parades of blue and lime green descended on the Emerald City on Sunday the eighth. Jovial chants percolated in the atmosphere, intermingled with a hope that seemed to be so rare in those days. In a spectacular display, the Seahawks won the Sixtieth Super Bowl. Its aftermath felt uplifting, like a sort of mayhem, like a state of euphoria.

Spring in Gold Bar

The Herb Farm welcomed the dawn of the bloom season with a flourishing of herbs and edible plants like daylilies, nasturtium, and Nootka rose. The restaurant offered a nine-course *prix fixe* menu themed "Valley of Eden." After all, paradise is but a garden of herbs and an orchard of trees — a celebration of milestones and a promise of things yet to come.

Willow's Lodge had a farm, a garden, and a little pen with two pet pigs. Beside it was the Sammamish River walking trail, which became lush with salmon, ducks, and sometimes, one or two great blue herons in the springtime. The month was March.

—

People emerged from hibernation, driving out of the city to spend the glorious sunbeam days outdoors. Streets slipped by in a blur of color from pink Yoshino cherry blossoms, orange trumpet honeysuckle, yellow Scotch broom, and purple empress trees.

Cars drove past Monroe, past Sultan, heading in the direction of Steven's Pass. Beside the US-2 was a small park on the edge of the Skykomish River. Nature was pervaded with giants — Douglas fir, western redcedar, and vine maple. Beneath them sprang shrubs of orange salmonberry, red bearberry, and white snowberry. Pacific bleeding heart, miner's lettuce, skunk cabbage, and yarrow bloomed on the ground of pebble and stone, while overhead, cars zipped by on a metal bridge suspended over the river. The month was April.

—

A small house stood on Lewis Avenue. It was navy-ship gray, with a low wooden fence and a front porch step that buckled from years of wear. Inside, the design was modern, contemporary, minimalist. There were cozy teal couches, soft white pin lights, and sturdy furniture made of wrought iron and reclaimed wood. Outside was a white Pathfinder.

At the back of the house was a deck with two Adirondack chairs and a fire pit between them. To the left was a Kousa dogwood, its flat white flowers in spring a prelude to crunchy red berries in summer. The back of the yard sloped up to a red barn house tucked in the corner. The next-door neighbor's meticulously cared-for plant boxes were visible over the fence, while the neighbor in the back had string lights across their yard that lit up like fireflies at night.

A handful of blocks away was a bar where the locals gathered. It had a pool table, a foosball table, a poker table, and a space for live music on special occasions. In the distance, the alpenglow of Mount Index was visible on a clear day. Overhead, a sea of stars shone bright on a clear night. The month was May.

Summer in Bellingham

The train line in Gold Bar passes through Bellingham eighty-eight miles to the northwest. They are distant, incongruent places, yet still connected by the artery of a single railway. One could daydream about stowing away on a freight car like a vagabond traveler. The month was June.

—

The month was July. The bustling college town was teeming with art, culture, and cuisine. At the intersection of two busy streets was The Pickford, an independent local theater. Nearby was the Federal Building on Magnolia Street, built in the style of the Second Italian Renaissance Revival. A few steps away was Mount Baker Theater on Commercial Street, a beautifully restored architectural treasure for performing arts.

Some streets were lined with tidy restaurants, others with rows of well-maintained houses, most built around a century ago. Small herds of deer idly roamed the neighborhoods. A young buck non-chalantly crossed between two yards. Perhaps he was heading to

Fairhaven to visit Le Chat Noir, Mambo Italiano, or one of the local boutiques.

Boats docked in the busy seaport. Captains and their crews frequented Nicki's Bella Marina, Anthony's Hearthfire Grill, and the handful of taverns near the harbor. On the other side, Hotel Bellwether hosted family picnics, live concerts, and outdoor barbecues in the firework months. A harbor seal bobbed up and down, industriously working for her catch of the day.

—

In this place, mountains meet sea meet islands. A lenticular stack hovered over the Twin Sisters. From Oyster Dome, one could see the San Juan Islands. In the glittering water, a ferry from Anacortes was inching toward Friday Harbor, with its collection of art galleries, gift shops, a whale museum, and old stone lime kilns as big as houses — the remnants of a bygone era. The month was August.

—

For now, Doris the Disco Duck, a silver mirror-ball statue, lived in Little Squalicum Park on Marine Drive, where dogs were allowed to roam leash-free. Summer days were always conducive to leisurely walks on the pier that overlooked Bellingham Bay. One could spend their whole day in the beautiful surroundings, where manmade structures met natural wonder. Everything was in balance.

Like crepuscular mammals that are most active at dawn and dusk, the Salish sea and sky are at their most vibrant in the turning hours. In the exchange between day and night, their colors, movements, and shapes shift and radiate brilliance.

The month was September. Summer's end was marked by the Sea Feast Fishing Festival, like the closing of a chapter. Nirvana was a drive back to Hoff Way in the twilight hours, after all the commotion was done.

Fall in Vancouver, British Columbia

Further north past Mount Vernon, past Burlington, and past the Peace Arch at the Douglas border crossing between Blaine and Surrey, Vancouver greeted fall. Fright Night screamed to life at Playland in Hastings Park. Street attendants guided cars to on-street parking. Inside the venue was a cacophony of haunted houses, night rides, attractions, and food stands. Here, for a short time, adults could act like children again — carefree and unjaded.

A chill signified the incoming wave of the final months of the year. Torrents of cold rain and mist cascaded through the night air, dampening the mood of parkgoers. Still, they stormed the amusement park for a night of Halloween fun. From the Ferris wheel high above, Vancouver glowed with the electric haze of fluorescent lights.

—

A very special property, The Pan Pacific Hotel, stood in Coal Harbour like a shimmering beacon. Breakfast was served in an exclusive lounge for guests of the Pacific Club Suites. It offered panoramic views of the harbor, with its bicycle loops, walkways, parks, seaplane hangars, and buildings, like the one that housed Cactus Club Café.

The month was October. Canadian Thanksgiving and Columbus Day shared its second Monday, so Canadians were out and about for the long weekend. It was a short walk to Gastown, where the Pour House pub was located. The Mariners were playing the Bluejays on TV, while outside, the Rain City pulsated with life in the autumn season. The Gastown Steam Clock, resembling a Victorian-style street fixture, counted the seconds.

The clock doesn't tick backward. A year seems like a long time, but a person gets only an unknown, finite number of them. Downtown, Le Crocodile by Rob Feenie, a fixture in fine dining, was getting ready for their dinner service.

—

Along the Skykomish River, a stretch of road unfolded like a Van Gogh come to life. The scenic route was enveloped in the rustic hues and golden tones of fall. Farther on lay Steven's Pass, where the snow had begun to collect for mountain skiers. But for the moment, Oktoberfest was still in full swing in the Bavarian town of Leavenworth where the Fairbridge Inn was fully occupied. After the festivities, people would part and go their separate ways.

Fall is for endings. Perhaps they would all meet each other again in a season or a year. November was almost upon them once again. Everything happens for a reason, for a season.

Soon, it would be back to a world of facts and figures, people and pressure, rules and responsibilities. But for now, all that existed was this twenty-four-foot-wide road. Basked in the amber impermanence of fall, the Pathfinder sped off in the distance.

The years flow, from the chill of winter,

To the thaw of spring,

To the radiance of summer,

To the eventide of fall, when the cycle begins anew.

Afterword

Hello to you, dear reader, out there somewhere in the world. I would like to sincerely thank you for taking the time to read this book. I started it as a project with the goal of writing twenty-five stories in twenty-five weeks. Half a year later, I achieved this milestone.

Here is a timeline of events.

January to June 2025

I started journaling in the first half of 2025 as a form of therapy. I wrote around thirty thousand words about different topics pertaining to migration, society, and philosophy. This time of introspection, as well as simply experiencing life, informed my writing.

My experiences from the last few years included fostering cats, the disastrous trip to Florida, and the various incidents with scams, grants, insurances, and taxes. I read about the store that closed on the news. Beyond reflection, I found no other purpose or reason for what I had written.

Between February and May, I had the experiences I recounted in "The Demented Dentist of Mira Mesa", "Whales Outside Our Windows", "Who Looks Inside", and "Zorro at the Balboa".

I spent a lot of time writing in the place on Ash Street, Better Buzz, and Pappalecco.

July to December 2025

A new business opportunity ("Sugar and Salt") in the second half of the year got the ball rolling. Though the business deal did not close, it did inspire me to write about the encounter. This ignited my interest, motivated me to continue writing, and set the tone for the rest of the stories.

I reworked the stories about society and connected them with the stories about philosophy (and what I learned from each of them.) I found some surprising synchronicities. There were overlaps between what I thought were disparate topics. Even different philosophies touched on similar themes, such as human suffering.

Between July and December, I lived the events that inspired "Birdsong, Bramble, Time for Tea", "Little Dog That Could", and much of "A Year in the Pacific Northwest". In December, I attended the "Good Luck Reunion". On the way home, something clicked. I connected that event to what I read about midlife, then connected that to what I read about the U-shape of happiness. This is just an example of what the writing process has been like for me.

I divided my time writing between the place in Le Chardonnay, the local library, and the Starbucks inside Barnes & Noble. I was inspired by the thousands of books that surrounded me — the works of thousands of authors across time and space.

Substack (October 2025 to March 2026)

I posted my first Substack in the last week of October, and this venue for writing allowed me to express what I wanted to say and understand what I wanted to do. I then made a post every Monday between October and March. I would write short notes on my phone, type the words on my computer, and flesh out the stories in a quiet space.

Some stories bled to other stories, while others were ultimately abandoned. Some were long, continuous processes that required several weeks. The stories about investing and financial planning ("Money and Time" and "Fifteenth Day of the Month") summarize what I have learned about those topics. Events in February inspired me to write "The Dragonfly" and "Harbor from the Storms".

Substack's format led to several breakthroughs through compartmentalization. It also allowed me to hone my message and make my writing more coherent.

Book (February to June 2026)

The ultimate goal was to publish a book which I then worked on for the next five months.

In February, I completed my initial manuscript. I arranged the stories into chapters to make them more cohesive and flow better. I prepared the other parts of the book, all while simultaneously writing, editing, adding, cutting, and moving around different sections.

Between March and May, I signed agreements and worked with a proofreader, a copyeditor, and a book designer/illustrator. It was a relatively quick timeline, all in a few busy months. Looking back, I see how all the stars aligned.

Now

All of these bring us to this present moment, with said book in your hands or device. I didn't set out to write a book about examining different philosophies initially, but this is exactly what it ended up being — such is life's journey.

The Two Oceans is the culmination of eighteen months of work and a distillation of a lifetime's worth of personal knowledge. Writing this book has lifted me up from the dark sea of depression and anxiety. It is my hope that in sharing this, it might find its way to others who need solace and a sense of kinship.

I plan on posting on Substack again, perhaps not right away, but soon. I would very much appreciate your reading or subscribing to me there. Perhaps, that is also where I will plant the seeds for a third book.

That is all for now. I wish you all the best, and I hope to write to you again soon!

Acknowledgments

This book is a mosaic of the experiences I had and, more notably, the people I met along the way:

Barış Şehri (*sehribookdesign.com*), a true "book whisperer", for the cover and interior design, illustrations, and typography. Thank you for bringing my ideas to life and giving my book its visual identity. I am in awe of your artistic vision and creative sensibilities.

Susan Gaigher (*self-publishingstudio.com*), the hero of this book, for the copyedit. Thank you for agreeing to work on my manuscript at the eleventh hour. I was confident it was in safe hands based on the first time we worked together. Once again, I am honored to have your magic touch, making the words I wrote truly sing. I learned so much from you throughout this process.

Joe Pierson, for the proofread. Thank you for catching and checking the "fine print" in a timely turnaround. I am grateful for your meticulous eye for detail. Jeff Rodgers, for lending me your ear and patiently listening to my problems. Thank you for being a therapist and a friend.

Alex L. Konicke (*alexkonicke.com*) and Jeffrey D. Briggs (*jeffreydbriggs.com*), for the foreword and testimonial, respectively. I appreciate your kindness and generosity with your time and contributions to this book, which make it so much more special. Your deft prose as writers and keen senses as authors inspire me.

Doug, for inviting me to go on some of your adventures, some of which became part of this book. Kevin, Pam, Rick, and Stephen, for starting your own Substacks and, in the process, giving me the idea to start one too. Andy, Aurora, Daisy, Dominic, Edna, Elara, Immaculate, Jay, Joseph, Kris, Lucinda, Mariah, Mel, Rachielle,

Raquel, Steven, Vanessa, and Virginia, for following me on Substack and, unknowingly, being the test readers of this book. Thank you.

—

In science, there exist fundamental physical constants that define the limits of the universe. The speed of light and the strength of gravity are two such constants, interconnected through Einstein's theories of relativity, which define how space and time behave.

My mom and dad, Marilyn (finance) and Perfecto (business), for being the two constants in my life for more than forty years. Thank you both — for my past, my future, and my present. I am the person I am because of you. It is my greatest pleasure to share this world with you and to see it through all its changes.

About The Author

Martin Tiongson resides in the breathtaking state of Washington — an ideal, idyllic, and inspiring place for writing. His first book was about business. His second book was about philosophy. He has designs for a third sometime in the future. The logical progression is fiction, most likely.

Substack: *martintiongson.substack.com*
Goodreads: *goodreads.com/martintiongson*
LinkedIn: *linkedin.com/in/martintiongson*

"Tiongson's narrative is refreshingly honest, often challenging conventional business wisdom and providing practical insights into problem-solving and resilience. His storytelling is both accessible and engaging, making complex business concepts relatable to aspiring entrepreneurs and seasoned professionals alike." – IndieReader

"It's a light, easy read, and he doesn't get into too much technical business jargon. *Something to Be Proud Of* will suit anyone who wants to buy or improve their small business. ★★★★★" - Readers' Favorite

"Tiongson distils complex business principles into digestible wisdom: the importance of documentation, the art of supplier relationships, and the necessity of aligning passion with practicality. These lessons transcend industry boundaries, making the memoir a valuable resource for readers from diverse backgrounds. ★★★★★" - Reedsy Discovery

SOMETHING

TO BE

PROUD OF

A MEMOIR ON SMALL BUSINESS
AND THE BIGGER BUSINESS OF PURSUING ONE'S PASSION

MARTIN TIONGSON

www.ingramcontent.com/pod-product-compliance
Lightning Source LLC
LaVergne TN
LVHW100301210926
848480LV00003B/993